YOUR FAMILY, GOD'S WAY

YOUR FAMILY, GOD'S WAY

Developing and Sustaining Relationships in the Home

Wayne A. Mack

P&R PUBLISHING
P.O. BOX 817 • PHILLIPSBURG • NEW JERSEY 08865-0817

All Scripture quotations, unless otherwise noted, are from the New American Standard Bible. Copyright 1960, 1962, 1963, 1968, 1971, 1972, 1973, 1975, 1977, by the Lockman Foundation. Moody Press.

Scripture references marked NIV are from the New International Version. Copyright 1973, 1978, 1984, International Bible Society. Holman Bible Publishers.

All personal illustrations in this book, with the exception of those from my own life and family, have been "flattened out," the names of individuals having been changed and certain identifying features withheld to protect the confidentiality of the people involved. Though factually based, many illustrations are composites of actual situations I have encountered among couples and families I have counseled over a span of many years.

Library of Congress Cataloging-in-Publication Data

Mack, Wayne A.
    Your family, God's way : developing and sustaining relationships
in the home / Wayne A. Mack.
        p.   cm.
    ISBN 0-87552-358-7
    1. Family—Religious life. 2. Communication in the family.
I. Title.
BV4526.2.M244 1991
248.8'45—dc20   91-27911

Contents

Preface

In a newspaper article some time ago Marshall Auerbach, a lawyer from Illinois, lamented the high rate of divorce in the United States.

Over the last 30 years I have participated in the break-up of more marriages than I care to remember. I'm a divorce lawyer by profession—I wrote the divorce law for the state of Illinois—but I'm a romantic at heart, so I suffer pangs of sympathy for both parties during the dissolution process. In fact, I make a strenuous effort to reconcile them before they take that final step, and I can tell you that it's becoming more difficult in the last 10 years.

Since 1960 about 40 million people have been divorced. A marriage counselor I know calls divorce "the death of a dream." She is convinced that had Romeo and Juliet lived today in her Chicago suburb, it is likely they would have visited her office for help in preserving their marriage.

How does one explain the magnitude of marital destruction that has allowed us to label the 80's "the age of divorce"? The statistics are shocking. This nation is awash in divorce.

Divorce is big business, by some estimates a "multibillion dollar industry." According to the *Wall Street Journal*, there were 700 divorce lawyers practicing 10 years ago. Now there are 11,000.

What is the condition of marriages today? In the last decade marriages have been breaking up at the rate of nearly 1.2 million a year. Over time, that amounts to the dissolution of a high percentage of marriages and a lot of people going through divorce. Add to that the fact that many marriages legally intact are plagued with problems. Many marriages (Christian and non-Christian) that never

vii

make it to the divorce court are falling far short of God's design for marriage and family life as presented in the Bible.

The truth is that no marriage (including mine and yours) fully approximates God's design. As I write this book, my wife and I have been married for thirty-four years. We have four biological children and two daughters-in-law who are all professing Christians. By God's grace, we have enjoyed good marriage and family relationships. This side of heaven, however, we will always see room for improvement.

I suggest that what is true of our family is also true of yours. Your family life can always be better. When we see pride, complacency, apathy, status-quoism in our families, it indicates that they are deteriorating or soon will be. When we think there's nothing more we can learn, there's no more progress we can make.

What this means is that building our families God's way should be a matter of great concern to us. All other ways are destined ultimately to fail. After all, marriage and family are God's idea. He originated these relationships. He planned them to be among the greatest blessings a person could have. He created the first man and woman, who became the first married couple and parents. He introduced them to each other. He gave them their premarital counseling and then performed the first wedding service. God, the originator, knows how a marriage and family should function. He fully understands the family's potential for delight or disaster. He is the ultimate marriage and family therapist.

This book is an attempt to explain God's principles for a better family. In it you will find Bible truths about good family relations explained, exercises for evaluating yourself and your family in the light of these truths, and practical guidelines for implementing the biblical principles. I encourage you to anticipate God's blessing on you and your family as you consider building your family *God's way*. God's promise is that those who hear and obey his Word will be blessed (Luke 11:28). So dig in and expect a blessing from God!

As you read this material and complete the assignments at the close of each chapter, open yourself to the ministry of the Holy Spirit. Ask him for honesty, openness, insight, desire, and power to receive and do whatever he asks. Keep in mind that true prosperity and success in a biblical sense are promised to those who do what the Bible says (Josh. 1:8; Ps. 1:1-3). Don't forget that those who are united by faith to Jesus Christ are new creatures, having new power to put off unbiblical patterns and put on more biblical lifestyles (2 Cor. 5:17; Eph. 5:17-24; Phil. 2:12, 13).

If this book should make you aware of areas or ways in which God wants you to change, be assured that for a Christian this is exciting. Be confident that God will help you as you trust in him. You must work, but you must work in faith. Depend wholly on God to enable you to do what pleases him. Be aware that what pleases God will ultimately please you. God is able and willing to help you. You can count on that.

Acknowledgments

I gratefully acknowledge the help of many people in the preparation of this book. To Beth Mack, Judith McKenzie, Harold McKenzie, and Irma Longworth I extend my appreciation for their skillful typing and retyping of the manuscript. My wife and children deserve much credit for all they have taught me during the years as we have sought to learn how to practice family living God's way. I am also indebted to Geraldine Irwin, Dr. John Neal (one of my counseling colleagues), Karen Hoffner, and especially Susan Lutz and Thom Notaro for their editorial work. They have applied the editorial scalpel to my wordy manuscript and have pared it down to what is hopefully a more readable and helpful publication. I also want to recognize Dr. Kenneth Hurst (a fellow worker at CCEF) for the encouragement he gave me to persevere in completing this work for publication. Finally, I want to thank Bryce Craig of Presbyterian and Reformed Publishing Company for his willingness to publish this book and several others I have written.

PART ONE

THE GROUNDWORK FOR GOD-HONORING FAMILY RELATIONSHIPS

1

First Things First—
The Maximum Husband and Father

When most people looked at Greg (a pseudonym), they saw all the marks of success. He was a well-dressed, intelligent, articulate man with an attractive and accomplished wife and two gifted children. At forty he was already very wealthy. Besides that, he was an outstanding leader in his church. Greg seemed the model of a successful man.

Yet there he was—sitting with his wife across from me in my counseling office. Ostensibly they were there to seek counsel on how to deal with a troublesome relative, but it soon became evident that their real problem was with each other. Greg may have appeared a success in many areas of life, but in one vital dimension he was not doing well. He and his wife both agreed that he was seriously deficient as a husband and father.

His wife was hurting badly and felt estranged from him. "I admire him greatly," she acknowledged, "but I don't feel that he really cares for me or respects me. He doesn't let me get close to him. I want us to share with each other more, especially about spiritual matters. But it just doesn't happen." By Greg's own admission, their relationship was stagnating because of things he had done or failed to do. He confessed, "My wife is a very godly, caring, cooperative person. The fault is primarily mine."

Greg and his wife were not sharpening one another or stimulating one another to love and good works (Prov. 27:17; Heb. 10:24, 25). In his relationship with his children there was little if any emotional closeness. He was not deeply involved in bringing them up in the instruction (counsel) and discipline of the Lord. By default, that had become primarily his wife's responsibility. His influence in their lives was minimal. In fact, as the children moved into their teenage years, the distance between them seemed to widen.

Greg represents hundreds of men I know and thousands I have never met. Perhaps he represents you. You may or may not be as successful as he is in the business world, but you are like him in that you are a professing Christian who wants to be a better husband and father.

The Key

In this chapter, I want to share with you God's perspective on the most important factor in becoming a maximum husband and father. God sees this factor as the key to making a man a powerful blessing to his family. It was this element that was missing in Greg's life.

What is this key factor? Psalm 128:1-4 describes it for us: "How blessed is everyone who fears the Lord, who walks in His ways. When you shall eat of the fruit [labor] of your hands, you will be happy and it will be well with you. Your wife shall be like a fruitful vine, within your house, your children like olive plants around your table. Behold, for thus shall the man be blessed who fears the Lord."

Here we have a picture of the various members in God's kind of family: what they are like, how they function, how they relate to one another, and what empowers and motivates them to be the family they are. In this chapter we will consider what the psalm teaches about the husband and father. In the next two chapters we will focus on its description of the wife and mother and the children.

The Benefits of Fearing God

This psalm indicates that to be God's kind of husband and father, you must be a man who fears God (vv. 1, 4). An appropriate fear of God will make you an unusual blessing to your wife and children. It will make you attractive to your family. You will become an effective husband and father. The fear of God will be the soil out of which your positive influence will grow and the basic reason your family will arise and call you blessed. I encourage you to meditate on what the Bible says will happen to you as a God-fearing man.

God says that God-fearing people:

1. Receive divine instruction concerning the choices they should make (Ps. 25:12).

2. Are prosperous in the most important ways (Pss. 25:13; 112:3).

3. Experience God's goodness (Ps. 31:19).

4. Are special objects of God's protection (Ps. 31:20).

5. Have children to whom God shows compassion (Ps. 103:11-18).

6. Have descendants who will be great on the earth in the most important ways (Ps. 112:2).

7. Are motivated to be gracious and generous (Ps. 112:4, 5).

8. Will be confident, courageous people (Ps. 112:6-8; Prov. 14:26).

9. Will experience contentment (Ps. 112:5, 6, 9; Prov. 19:23).

10. Will be praying people whose prayers will be heard (Ps.145:19).

11. Are blessed with wisdom (Prov. 1:7; 9:10).

12. Are teachable and peaceful (Prov. 8:13; 14:26; 15:33; Acts 9:31).

13. Are characterized by integrity and faithfulness (Job 2:3).

14. Are considerate and kind (Ps. 112:4, 5).

15. Are noted for constructive speech (Mal. 3:16).

16. Are patient, hopeful, and genuine (Ps. 147:11).

17. Persevere in doing what is right (Ps. 112:3, 5; 2 Cor. 7:1).

18. Work hard, but are not so committed to work that they do not have time for enjoyment (Ps. 128:3).

19. Accept responsibility for their own families and yet are not overly responsible (Ps. 128:3).

20. Are devoted to their families and find them to be a source of great satisfaction (Ps. 128:1-4).

21. Delight in worshipping God (Rev. 14:7).

22. Love the Scripture and order their lives according to God's commands (Ps. 112:1; Eccl. 12:13).

How does all this apply to my friend Greg and his family problems? Certainly, he needed specific instructions on the issues involved in husbanding and fathering. In the course of counseling we discussed such issues in great detail. But Greg needed more than that. He needed a healthy, wholesome fear of God in his life.

What It Means to Fear God

What does it mean to be a God-fearing man? Unclear answers to this question will hinder you in building a better family God's way. Some people have a fear of God that is heavy, even oppressive. To them the thought of God brings anxiety, dread, or terror. Their fear of God is debilitating, a curse rather than a blessing. They think that God is out to get them, that he is petulant, vindictive, and hard to get along with.

An example of this kind of fear is found in the story Jesus told about the three men who had been given talents. Two men actively invested their talents and produced an increase. The third man did nothing with his talent. When called to give an account, he explained his inaction by saying, "I knew you to be a hard man, reaping where you did not sow, and gathering where you scattered no seed. And *I was afraid*, and went away and hid your talent" (Matt. 25:24, 25, emphasis added).

This man's fear rendered him powerless to act. He thought of his master as a vindictive despot who delighted in putting people on the spot and wreaking vengeance on them. Such a defeatest attitude reflects the outlook of many people today. They live in fear of other people, circumstances, or what may happen. They even view God in the way the man in our Lord's story viewed his master.

But the fear of Matthew 25:25 is not the fear of God described in Psalm 128. The one will impoverish you and your family; the other will enrich your life. Matthew 25:25 fear will cause you to be insecure, discontented, unforgiving, unloving, authoritarian, or spineless. But Psalm 128 fear produces the opposite effects. It is constructive, not destructive. It will draw you toward God, not drive you away from him. It will stimulate responsible action, not breed idleness. It will cause you to reach out, not pull in. It will help you serve others and diminish selfishness. And it will demolish other fears, which inhibit confident, joyful, fruitful living.

Scripture asserts that if you are in union with Christ Jesus, you have no reason to be held captive to a fear that involves the dread of God. If you have never experienced the forgiveness of God through Christ's redemption, you have every reason to be terrified of God because you have never made peace with him. But if you have trusted in Christ alone for salvation and forgiveness of sins, confessing him as Lord, the Bible says that you have no cause to be in bondage to this kind of fear. God has granted you the spirit of sonship and the right to call him your Father (Rom. 8:15). As a child of your loving, compassionate heavenly Father, you are an heir of God and a co-heir with Christ. You are destined to share Christ's glory (Rom. 8:17), having been declared righteous through his death, reconciled to God, and saved from God's wrath through him (Rom. 5:9, 10). Because of your relationship with Jesus, you don't have to be distraught by the thought of God. In fact, you now have every reason to rejoice in God, fearing him in the positive sense described in Psalm 128. And that leads us to ask exactly what it means for you to fear God.

Simply put, the fear of God is the inevitable response to a growing, biblical understanding of and relationship with the true and living God who has revealed himself in Jesus Christ.

The essence of the fear of God is vividly illustrated in the life of Moses in Exodus 15:1-18. Prior to this passage Moses had an experience that greatly enlarged his concept of God. The Lord had just miraculously and powerfully delivered his people from certain destruction at the hands of the Egyptians. God had opened the waters of the Red Sea and allowed the relatively helpless and defenseless Israelites to pass to the other side in safety. He had dramatically thwarted the murderous intentions of the powerful Egyptians. God had clearly shown his might, power, and loving-kindness to his people. As a result, Moses was gripped by the excellency of who God is. Moses had encountered God as one who is highly exalted, majestic in power, glorious in holiness, fearful (awesome) in praises, unfailing in faithfulness, completely trustworthy, abundant in mercy, committed to his people, absolutely and eternally sovereign, and unrivalled in excellence.

His reflex response to this pervasive awareness was adoration, love, and obedience. Every area of his being was now controlled by a big concept of God. He experienced what Psalm 128 calls "the fear of God."

Abraham's life provides us with another powerful illustration of what it means to be a God-fearing man. The Bible calls Abraham God's friend. He undoubtedly had a close relationship with God. Moreover Abraham had an exalted concept of God that influenced his personal and family life in very practical ways. His relationship to God was the most significant factor in his life.

Abraham's life cannot be understood apart from his big concept of God. On occasion, the Bible indicates, that concept receded, but the overall picture is that of a man whose fear of God was preeminent, pervasive, and powerful. Because he feared God, he was willing to leave his homeland and move to an entirely new area. Because he feared God, he was a magnanimous man, willing to give the best land to his nephew Lot. Because he feared God, he was content with what he had, unwilling to take advantage of others, concerned about justice (the rights of others), and willing to risk his own life and expend time, effort, and finances for the sake of his family. He chose to put God's will before everything else, including his own feelings and desires. Abraham's big concept of God made him the godly man that he was.

The Motivating Power of the Fear of God

A healthy, wholesome fear of God will do the same for you and me. An all-encompassing sense (1) of the presence of God, (2) of the unrivalled majesty of God, (3) of the abundant mercy and grace of God, (4) of the faithfulness of God, (5) of your dependence on and responsibility to God, (6) of your relationship with God and the priority of that relationship, (7) of the supreme perfection of God will redirect every aspect of life. It will call forth a loving and unreserved commitment to God. It will propel you to structure your life, order your affairs and relationships, and make decisions according to God's will. You will be a man who walks with God in close fellowship. Your life will revolve around him so that you can say with Paul, "For to me to live is Christ." You will be stimulated and empowered to relate to your wife and family in a God-ordained way. You will become the blessed (happy) man of Psalm 128, who in turn becomes a blessing to his wife and children. Building a family God's way will not remain "the impossible dream." It will become a reality.

Acquiring and Maintaining the Fear of God

This leads us very naturally to the question, How can a healthy fear of God be acquired and maintained? Ultimately, it is possible only if you have been born again in Jesus Christ. Left to yourself, you may fear God in the stifling, destructive way previously described. It takes no special work of God in your life for you to be terrified of God. But to fear God in the proper way is a different matter. This requires a gracious work of God in your life. The Holy Spirit must enable you to be spiritually reborn and redeemed from sin through the work of Jesus Christ.

Speaking to this issue, Peter challenges us to live our lives in reverent fear, because we know that we have been redeemed through the precious blood of Christ (1 Pet. 1:17-19). Peter seems to be saying that our redemption in Christ provides a twofold reason to fear God: (1) It should inspire a big concept of God because of the means by which he has saved us. We have been loosed from the penalty and power of our sin by nothing less than the death of God's own Son, Jesus Christ. (2) Peter asserts that Christ's redemption includes a deliverance from our old way of life, in which a reverent fear of God was lacking (Rom. 3:18).

By now you may be thinking, "I'm a Christian, but the fear of God is not very powerful in my life." That was Greg's problem. He had confessed Jesus Christ as his Lord and Savior. He wanted to please God. But his fear of God was minimal, and his relationship with him was superficial. In such a case, what else do you need in order to develop a more vital awareness of the true and living God in your life?

God's word to us through Jeremiah provides important insight into this matter: "They will be my people, and I will be their God. I will give them singleness of heart and action, so that they will always fear me for their own good and the good of their children after them. . . . I will never stop doing good to them, and I will inspire them to fear me . . ." (Jer. 32:38-40, NIV).

Note carefully what this passage says about the fear of God. God's people—those who belong to him—are without exception God-fearing people. They fear him because God inspires them to do so and not because of any natural inclination. *He* gives them singleness of heart and action. Paul recognized this and wrote that "God, who said, 'Let light shine out of darkness,' made his light shine in our hearts to give us the light of the knowledge of the glory of God in the face of Christ" (2 Cor. 4:6, NIV). Paul is saying that we will never comprehend God's majesty and glory unless God turns on the light in the darkness of our hearts. He must provide illumination in our inner man if we are to understand his splendor.

The Prayer Factor

Because of this conviction, Paul frequently petitions God to reveal himself. In Ephesians, he writes, "I keep asking that the God of our Lord Jesus Christ, the glorious Father, may give you the Spirit of wisdom and revelation, so that you may know him better" (Eph. 1:17, NIV). Later in the same epistle he says, "I pray that you . . . may have the power . . . to grasp how wide and long and high and deep is the love of Christ, and to know this love that surpasses knowledge—that you may be filled to the measure of all the fulness of God" (Eph. 3:17-19, NIV).

Several important facts should be observed in these passages. These are prayer petitions addressed to God, though shared with the readers of the epistle. Paul is not directly exhorting or admonishing his readers. He is praying. He is asking God to do something in their lives. Certainly, this implies that without God's help, we cannot experience whatever he is describing. In addition, I am struck by the fact that this particular prayer request was one that he frequently and continuously brought to God. He says, "I keep asking God . . ." (Eph. 1:17); "I pray . . ." (present tense), not "I prayed" (past tense)(Eph. 3:16).

When you study Paul's Ephesian prayers, you realize that they can be boiled down to only one thing. The focus of Paul's prayer was that God might give us wisdom and revelation so that we may know him better. To Paul, the fulfillment of this entreaty was the fountainhead that opened up a world of blessing. If you are a God-fearing man, you will pray because you fear God. And, as you pray aright, your wholesome fear of God will be nurtured and increased *because* you pray. This will be the dynamic that will enable you to build your family God's way.

Remember Greg? He wanted to be a good husband and father. He worked hard to give his family the very best. He really cared for them. Still, he had become aware that something was amiss in his relationships with his family and with God. Greg was so gifted and successful in most of what he did that he had become too self-sufficient. He was so busy that he neglected his prayer life. The telltale signs of this neglect were a distant relationship with God and a limited impact on his family. You can't develop a healthy, wholesome God-consciousness or build a family God's way without a meaningful prayer life. However, as important as prayer is in this connection, it is but one piece of the puzzle.

"Be Still and Know"

According to Psalm 46, to nurture a controlling and pervasive awareness of God you must "be still and know" that he is God (Ps. 46:10). That means regularly taking time out from your hurried pace of life to reflect on who and what God is. Psalm 46 depicts a man who is hopeful, secure, and courageous in the midst of unusually difficult circumstances. That is not his natural temperament. He has become that kind of man because he has taken time to "be still and know that [he] is God." I urge you to make it a regular priority to be still and meditate on God as he is revealed in Jesus Christ. Scripture declares that the glory of God is disclosed in the face of Jesus (2 Cor. 4:6). Christ "is the radiance of God's glory and the exact representation of his being" (Heb. 1:3, NIV). Spend time regularly reflecting on the person and work of Jesus Christ— who he is and what he did, what he is doing and will do. Seek to know him personally. Talk to him about whatever is on your mind.

Place yourself as an observer in the scenes described in the New Testament and try to picture what is happening. Consider how he lived and related to people, as well as what he did and said. Try to understand why he spoke and acted as he did. Imagine what he may have been thinking or feeling. Note how people responded to him.

See his majesty, his graciousness, his wisdom, his compassion, his righteousness and justice, his power. Go often to the cross on which he died for your sins. Proceed to the empty tomb from which he arose and was powerfully declared to be the Son of God. Spend time on the Mount of Olives from which he ascended to the presence of God the Father. Contemplate the throne room of God, where he sits possessing all authority over heaven and earth, making intercession for you and ruling over all things for the sake of the church. Consider what all this means for his relationship to the world, to people, to history—and to you.

Seek with Paul to know Christ more fully than you've ever known him to this point (Phil. 3:10). Don't be satisfied with a secondhand knowledge of Christ. I have encouraged people who have wanted to enhance their personal relationship with Jesus to have an hourly fellowship break. One man set his wrist watch alarm to sound off every hour. It reminded him to focus on Christ, talk to Him, and reflect on God's Word. This break became "the pause that refreshes" and helped him to develop a more God-conscious, Christ-centered life.

The Bible, God's Letter

Keep in mind that since the Bible is primarily a revelation of who and what God is, your relationship with God will be nourished by faithful meditation on God's Word. "The Scriptures . . . testify about me," Jesus said in John 5:39. David tells us that "the statutes of the Lord are trustworthy, making wise the simple. . . . The commands of the Lord are radiant, giving light to the eyes. The fear of the Lord is pure, enduring forever" (Ps. 19:7-9, NIV). Note that this passage closely connects God's Word with "the fear of the Lord." David does this because he knows that the inevitable response to a proper study of God's Word is an increased veneration of God. He realizes that those who consistently and submissively come to the Bible to meet God will not be disappointed. For the Bible is God's book (2 Tim. 3:16-17). In it God has revealed his attributes, his works, his concerns, his will, his intentions, his plans, his desires for his people, and his designs for the world that rejects him.

Develop the attitude that God is speaking to you as you read the Scriptures. Read them as you would a letter from your dearest friend. The two of you are making contact. You are coming to know your friend better. Receive what the Bible says as coming from your heavenly Father, your personal Savior and Lord, the great and awesome God of creation and redemption. Don't regard its teachings as abstract rules about life—mere duties to fulfill. Respond to God's Word as one who by grace has been brought into the family of the most wonderful person in all the universe. See everything in the Scripture as an invitation to enter into a deeper relationship with your majestic, infinite Father and Redeemer.

Christian counselors sometimes give people who are experiencing marital or family problems an assignment to make one graph depicting the high and low points of their relationship with God and another graph depicting the high and low points in their family relationships. Interestingly, when these two graphs are compared, the high and low points often coincide. Often when people sensed that their relationship with God was vital and deep, they also experienced a vital relationship with other family members.

Greg has been learning this basic lesson. Have you? If so, you're on track for building your family God's way. If not, I encourage you to repent, and by God's grace reorient your life to put first things first. It will do a world of good for you *and* your family.[1]

Study and Application Assignments

Do the assignments individually and then discuss your answers with your mate or your study group.

1. Reflect on (or if necessary, review) this chapter and answer the following questions:

   a. Describe in your own words the problem in Greg's life and how it was affecting his family.

   b. How does Psalm 128 describe the husband and father in God's kind of family? What is the one outstanding feature of this man's life as found in this Psalm?

   c. According to the Bible, why is a man's relationship with God so important for himself and his family? What benefits does God promise to the person (and his family) who makes his relationship with God a priority?

   d. What two types of "fear of God" were mentioned in the chapter? Describe the kind of fear of God that is destructive. What Bible example(s) illustrate this kind of fear? Can you think of some historical or contemporary examples of people who have had a destructive fear of God? How has this kind of fear affected their lives and families? Why have these people feared God in this way? Is such fear realistic for them? Is it warranted?

   e. Describe the kind of fear of God that is wholesome and constructive. How would you explain it to someone who doesn't have a biblical concept of the fear of God? What are its features? What Bible examples illustrate this fear of God? What effect do you think it had on their lives and families?

   f. Can you think of some historical or contemporary examples of people who have feared God in this constructive way? What effect has it had on their lives and families?

   g. What directives were given in this chapter about developing this healthy fear of God? Do you have any other suggestions about how a vital fear of God, i.e., relationship with him, may be maintained?

   h. Do you agree with the primary thesis of this chapter that a healthy relationship with God is the main factor in being God's kind of husband and father? Why or why not?

i. Evaluate your relationship with God at this time. (Excellent___, Good___, Fair___, Poor___, Nonexistent___.) Explain why you gave the rating you did. (If you have difficulty answering this and the next two questions, question 2 listed below should give you some help.)

j. Are you in practice, not just in theory, putting first things first? (Regularly___, Often___, Sometimes___, Seldom___, Never___.) Give reasons for rating yourself as you did.

k. Are there ways in which you should improve your relationship with God? (Yes___, No___, Maybe___.) If so, how?

2. Meditate on the twenty-two benefits listed in this chapter that are promised to the person who fears God. Consider what each of them means in practical, behavioral terms. Take each statement and ask yourself, Is this true in my life regularly (= 4), often (= 3), occasionally (= 2), seldom (= 1), never (= 0)? According to these statements, the fear of God will affect a man's life in certain ways. So, to some extent, you may use these benefits as a means of realistically evaluating the depth and condition of your relationship with God. After you have rated yourself on each of the twenty-two statements, make a list of all the items that you scored 0 or 1 or 2. Plan how you can improve your relationship with God. Perhaps you will want to write out a statement of commitment and sign your name to what you are going to do. Pray daily for God's help in making the desired improvements. Refer back to your list regularly as a means of continuous evaluation and motivation.

3. What do the following Bible verses reveal about Abraham's relationship with God, particularly his fear of God? Are there any indications about how Abraham's fear of God was developed and sustained? What impact did it have on his life and family? Try to gain specific insights about what you are doing or should do to develop your relationship with God and build your family God's way. As you look at each passage, ask yourself: What is God saying to me about my relationship with him? How should what I see here be applied to my life and family? How well am I doing in implementing the teaching(s) of this passage?

a. 2 Chronicles 20:7

b. Isaiah 41:8

c. James 2:23

d. Genesis 12:1-8

  e. Genesis 13:8, 9

  f. Genesis 14:14

  g. Genesis 14:22, 23

  h. Genesis 14:24

  i. Genesis 21:10, 11

  j. Genesis 22:11, 12

  k. Romans 4:19-21

4. Study the following verses and note what each of them teaches or implies about: (1) the excellence of God; (2) the fear of God; (3) what our relationship with God should be like; (4) what place God should have in our lives; (5) how to develop the fear of God; and (6) what happens to the person who fears God.

  a. Genesis 5:22

  b. Exodus 15:11

  c. Exodus 34:6, 7

  d. Deuteronomy 6:13; 10:12

  e. 2 Chronicles 20:6-19

  f. Psalm 19:7-11

  g. Psalm 34:7, 11

  h. Psalm 128:1

  i. Psalm 130:4

  j. Psalm 139:1-6

  k. Psalm 139:7-10

  l. Psalm 139:13-16

  m. Psalm 139:23, 24

  n. Psalm 147:11

  o. Proverbs 1:7

  p. Proverbs 8:13

  q. Proverbs 14:26, 27

  r. Proverbs 19:23

  s. Proverbs 28:14

  t. Isaiah 40:10-31

u. Matthew 10:28

v. Romans 8:26-39

w. Romans 11:36

x. Revelation 4:8-11

y. Revelation 5:9-14

z. Revelation 15:3, 4

5. Reflect on what you have just studied and write out your response to this question: What difference should all this make in my own life and family relationships?[2]

Notes

[1]For further study on the subjects of effective prayer, how to profit from your Bible, and developing your relationship with God, I recommend the following resources: *Knowing God,* J. I. Packer; *Trusting God,* Jerry Bridges; *Between Walden and the Whirlwind,* Jean Fleming; *Pray With Your Eyes Open,* Richard Pratt; *How to Pray Effectively,* Wayne Mack (tape); *The Practical and Profitable Use of the Bible* (tape), Wayne Mack; *Scriptural Meditation* (2 tapes), Wayne Mack. The books may be purchased from a Christian bookstore; books and tapes may be purchased from Biblical Counseling and Living Supplies, 2299 Brodhead Road, Bethlehem, Pa. 18017.

[2]Additional information with specific guidelines for husbands is found in three books by Wayne A. Mack: *Strengthening Your Marriage, A Homework Manual for Biblical Living,* vol. 2 (Phillipsburg, N.J.: Presbyterian and Reformed, 1977 and 1980), and *Preparing for Marriage God's Way* (Tulsa, Okla.: Hensley, 1986). Cassette tapes by Wayne Mack dealing with husband and wife relationships, sex relations, and finances are available. These study materials may be secured from Biblical Counseling and Living Supplies, 2299 Brodhead Road, Bethlehem, Pa. 18017.

2

Something's Happened to Sally—
The Fulfilled and Fulfilling Wife and Mother

As far back as Sally (a pseudonym) could remember, she had looked forward to being a wife and mother. Her greatest desire in life was to get married and have children.

When she was four years old, her mother and father divorced. Sally never saw her biological father again. Her mother soon remarried, but her relationship with her mother and stepfather was a distant one. A sad and lonely girl, Sally was ill at ease around other people. Feeling inferior, unwanted, and unappreciated, she longed for the day when she could get married and have a family of her own. Then she would belong. Then she would love and be loved.

Sally did marry at the age of seventeen. Soon after that, she had her first child. Within a few years, she had two more. She and her husband had both become Christians and were involved in a good church. Her husband was faithful, loving, and kind. His business was a challenge, but it was doing well.

Now Sally had the husband and family she had always desired. Yet she was not happy. Although she had what she had thought would bring her fulfillment, she still saw herself as a failure. She felt pressured, guilty, fearful, inadequate, and overwhelmed. She was adrift as a wife, mother, and person.

To deal with her distress, Sally launched into new areas of activity. A hard worker with many abilities, she secured a position of responsibility and became a career woman. She also became more active in the church and another Christian organization.

People looked to her as a woman who could get things done. Yet Sally was still discontented. Depression increasingly dominated her life.

Sally didn't want to continue as she was. She needed to change. And so she came asking for help to become a more fulfilled and fulfilling woman.

Help Wanted

Perhaps you can identify with Sally. You may not view yourself as negatively as she did. But you sense that something is missing. And you want help on how to be a fulfilled and fulfilling person, wife, and mother. Deep down you long for direction and affirmation about God's purpose for you and a clearer perspective on your role in building your family God's way.

Sally wanted that, and she got it. It has been several years since she first sought assistance. Since then, she has been in the process of becoming a different person. Today she is not nearly as driven, fearful, or unstable as she once was. Though at times still tempted in these areas, she has seen significant victory over her earlier problems.

Recently, Sally wrote me a note saying: "I'm glad to be able to tell you that my old friends [the distress and depression she had experienced] are no longer visiting me as they used to. I am much happier, secure and fulfilled."

What Happened to Sally?

What has made the difference? Sally is finding fulfillment and security in her deeper understanding of God's purpose for her as a person, wife, and mother. She is increasingly viewing herself from God's perspective, trying to structure her life according to God's directives. She realizes that she no longer has to be a superwoman, trying to attain some illusory goal. Now she has a clearer picture of what God wants her to be and do, and how that can be accomplished. And in that, she is finding fulfillment.

Obviously, I can't share everything Sally learned in counseling.

However, I am going to share some of the basic truths that she implemented, which helped her to get a new lease on life.

In the previous chapter we saw from Psalm 128 what God has to say about the husband and father in his role within the family. I want now to focus your attention on what God has to say in this psalm about the wife and mother. Real personal fulfillment (success) is a by-product of a God-centered life in which a person becomes and does what is pleasing to God.

God's Word to the Wife and Mother

God could have used hundreds of similes to describe the woman in the family, but he chose to describe her as a vine (Ps. 128:3). To us in the twentieth century, this may not seem like a very significant description. But to people living in Bible times, it was a different matter.

A vine had tremendous significance. It symbolized luxuriousness, value, and prosperity—something highly desirable and worthwhile. When God wanted to describe the good land into which he was going to bring his people, he said it would be a land with vines (Deut. 8:7, 8). When the king of Assyria tried to entice the people of Israel to submit to his reign, he promised that each one of them would have his own vine (Isa. 36:16). God dignified the vine concept by calling the nation of Israel, whom he brought into a unique relationship with himself, his vine (Jer. 2:21; Hos. 10:1). Jesus paid the ultimate compliment to the vine by calling himself the vine and by calling God the Father a vinedresser (John 15:1, 5).

From the context of John 15, it is evident that Jesus used the vine to describe himself because the vine symbolized life, refreshment, and ministry. Jesus is all of these things *par excellence:* "Without him we can do nothing" (John 15:5). We are absolutely dependent upon him as our source of life. He is our vine.

Could our Lord have paid the wife and mother a higher compliment? Could he have impressed us with her important home responsibilities in any better way? Women, God underscores your strategic ministry by comparing you to a vine.

Sally, the Vine

Sally needed to understand and really believe that biblical truth. From her childhood, she had thought of herself as unwanted, unworthy, and unacceptable to God, her family, or anyone else. She came for counseling still judging herself by her unbiblical standards of what makes a person worthwhile. Sally needed to accept the fact that God had made her a vine and given her a strategic ministry to her husband and children. Yes, she had sinned; yes, she had failed; yes, she was not the perfect wife or mother; yes, there was room for improvement. But as a redeemed sinner who was in union with Christ, sharing his life and indwelt by the Holy Spirit, her life had significance and potential. God called her a vine, and Sally needed to grasp the implications of that word for her life.

God's Word was saying that in some ways she was to her family what Christ is to his people. Certainly not in the absolute and fullest sense. Yet her ministry was to be a reflection of Christ's ministry. That made her important, and so it is with every wife and mother.

The Fruitful Vine

Notice in Psalm 128 that God not only calls a wife and mother to be a vine, he calls her to be a *fruitful* vine (Ps. 128:3). Some vines never benefit anyone or anything. They may look good, but they never bear fruit. They just take up space and require a lot of attention. They even divert nutrients away from other plants and may pass diseases on to others.

Women, God has put you in the world and in your family to be productive, to make an important contribution, to be a fruitful vine. At the time of creation, God said to the man and woman, "Be fruitful and increase in number; fill the earth and subdue it. Rule over the fish of the sea and the birds of the air and over every living creature that moves on the ground" (Gen. 1:28, NIV). Note carefully that God gave this command to the man *and* the woman. Woman was to be man's partner in being fruitful, in ruling the earth. Later God said of the woman that she was a suitable helper for man (Gen. 2:18). We know that the word translated "helper" does not suggest the idea of inferiority because it is joined to the word often translated "meet," which could be translated "corresponding to," "suitable," or "appropriate." The woman is to be a helper who *corresponds* to the man. She fits. She is capable. She stands with man and helps him to accomplish what he could never accomplish on his own. She adds dimensions that are equally important. Together they make an able team to accomplish, through God's strength, what he has purposed for them.

It's interesting to note that this word used of the woman is often used of God in Scripture (Deut. 33:29; Pss. 25:9; 121:1, 2). Because of who and what God is, he is the very "helper" we need. We can't get along without him. And because of who and what the woman is by divine creation, she is the very helper man needs to fulfill his God-given responsibilities in the world and in the home.

The Nature of the Fruit

If all that is so, what kind of fruit does God want you to bear? God fills in the details in numerous Bible passages.

Certainly the fruit of the Spirit described in Galatians 5:22-23 is part of this fruitfulness. God wants your life to be filled with love, joy, peace, patience, kindness, goodness, faithfulness, gentleness, and self-control. When Jesus said, "By this is my Father glorified, that you bear much fruit" (John 15:8), he was speaking primarily of the fruit of the Spirit. As you bear spiritual fruit, others see the power and glory of God manifested in your life.

In God's kind of family, a wife and mother must be more concerned about being than doing, more concerned about what she is than how she performs. Christian conduct is rooted in Christian character. Therefore your impact for God and your helpfulness to others depends on the work of the Spirit in your own life.

Peter emphasizes the same thought when he says to wives: "Be submissive to your husbands so that, if any of them do not believe the word, they may be won over without words by the behavior of their wives, when they see the purity and reverence of your lives. Your beauty should not come from outward adornment, such as braided hair and the wearing of gold jewelry and fine clothes. Instead, it should be that of your inner self, the unfading beauty of a gentle and quiet spirit, which is of great worth in God's sight. For this is the way the holy women of the past who put their hope in God used to make themselves beautiful" (1 Pet. 3:1-5, NIV).

Peter is pointing out that the most effective way to be fruitful in your family is by way of your life. All of your attempts to help your husband will be in vain unless your life demonstrates Christian character—the reality of Christ in you.

The "Fruitful Vine" Woman

Perhaps no passage gives us more insight into what it means to be a "fruitful vine" kind of wife and mother than Proverbs 31:10-31. Here is an example for all women who desire God's kind of family.

Her husband and children respect her greatly and rise up in public to praise her (v. 28). Her life impacts theirs in a way that they appreciate. And her influence reaches far beyond her home, into society. She is recognized, respected, and appreciated in all her surroundings. The world is a better place because of her (vv. 16, 20, 24, 31).

Certain details of this portrait cannot be applied directly to women in developed countries today for at least two reasons. First, some of the details no longer describe today's world. In verse 16, for example, buying and planting a field was more characteristic of life in an agrarian society. Likewise, the distaff and spindle were common in homes of that day (v. 19). Second, this woman evidently possessed some resources not available to everyone—then or now. She had servant girls (v. 15), money with which to buy a field, and rich clothing (vv. 16, 21, 22).

But the general principles found in this account are universally applicable. The character and conduct of this woman stand as a marvelous example of the wife and mother in God's kind of family. She is in some ways an example of what every Christian should be.

Characteristics of a "Fruitful Vine" Wife and Mother

Let's be more specific and look at what it means to be a "fruitful vine" wife and mother. According to verse 30, the fruitful vine is a woman who fears the Lord. She is a God-centered person. Like the husband of Psalm 128, she has a big concept of God—an accurate, growing, all-pervasive awareness of the true and living God. To her, God is a powerful reality. Whatever good there is in her flows out of her big concept of God. He is her everything—her motivating force, her strength, her hope, her counselor. The secret of her fruitfulness is not her dynamic personality, her strong will power, her physical beauty, her pleasant situation, her unusual resources, her good training, her natural gifts, or her exceptional husband or children. Her admirable life stems from her vital and deep relationship with God.

The Impossible Dream?

Maybe you have read the Proverbs 31 passage and declared it to be unrealistic, impossible. If so, you've assumed that you are dependent upon yourself to develop this kind of life. Looking to your past, your present, your resources, and your situation, you've said, "No way." That's because you've failed to realize that your sufficiency is of God, and that becoming this kind of person is the product of a close, personal relationship with God. Apart from that, you will be overwhelmed by what you read.

That is what had happened to Sally. She had a high view of her responsibilities, an oppressive sense of duty. She was driven toward perfection without even knowing what that was. All she knew was that she *should*—and yet could never—attain her mythical standard. Her pattern had been: trying hard to measure up, then judging herself to have failed, then collapsing in frustration and weariness. She would then rebound, roll up her sleeves, and go through the whole process again and again. Repeating this scenario over the years had led to discouragement, disillusionment, despair, and depression.

Sally professed to be a Christian, but her relationship with God was not very dynamic. In fact, she was works-oriented in her attitude toward God. Two of the biggest words in her vocabulary were "do" and "go." She was burdened by the fact that she was failing God as well as her family.

Having been involved in a Bible preaching church, she knew something of Bible teaching. Intellectually she knew the truth that God justifies (declares us to be righteous and credits to our account the merits of Christ) by grace (unmerited favor) through the person and work of Christ alone. But on a practical level, it meant very little in terms of how she thought and lived. Sally feared God, but mostly in the negative sense of seeing him as a hard taskmaster who demanded impossible things of her, and stood ready to pounce when she failed. She knew conceptually that for Christians, God is a gracious, glorious, and compassionate heavenly Father. But in the nitty-gritty of life her focus was on her *duty*.

As a result her relationship with God was impersonal and joyless. She knew little of that big, wholesome concept of God that enriches and empowers. Trying to produce the fruit of the Christian life without cultivating its root, she was starting where she should have finished.

When Sally gained new insights into the Christian life and her relationship with God, she began to experience a new kind of liberty. As she has made knowing God her number one priority, she has discovered a new sense of meaning, acceptance, power, and security. And she is much more fulfilled.

Proverbs 31 Priorities

A careful reading of Proverbs 31 presses us to one conclusion. A God-fearing wife and mother is a family-oriented person. Psalm 128 says she is a fruitful vine within the house. Proverbs 31 emphasizes that this woman takes excellent care of her family. Though clearly not restricted to the home (vv. 13, 14, 16, 20), she is utterly devoted to her family as her number-one ministry. Her family is not neglected while she does other important things.

"Her husband has full confidence in her" (v. 11, NIV), or as the New American Standard Bible puts it, "The heart of her husband trusts in her." He knows she is committed to him, and he trusts her without reservation. This means he depends upon her for support and help, knowing that he will not look in vain. The Hebrew verb found in this phrase literally means "to lean upon." It implies that this woman is dependable. When her husband needs a listening ear, when he is weary and discouraged, he knows she will be a refuge for him. When he shares his fears, his dreams, his joys, his problems, he is confident that she will not ridicule or reject him for having them. He can count on her to be lovingly honest with him. Her husband knows that he can depend on her prayer support as he faces the challenges and responsibilities of life. She is his fountain to whom he may look for refreshment. She enriches and excites his life. She does not delight in hurting him, but is always ready to lend assistance (vv. 11, 12, 23, 28). She is without question a husband-oriented person.

Her husband's public praise attests to his approval of how she relates to him. He values her more than all the women in the world (vv. 28, 29). She has not neglected him or the family while pursuing her own interests. Sensitive, available, and trustworthy, she has been a fruitful vine.

The passage also says a lot about this woman's relationship with her children. We read that her children rise up and bless her. Along with her husband they say, "Many daughters have done nobly, but you excel them all" (v. 29). They would not be saying that if she were grumpy, petulant, moody, bitter, or manipulative. They are impressed by her godliness, manifested in noble character and conduct. And they appreciate the way she has devoted herself to her family.

The Superwoman Cistern

Sally needed to get this perspective on her family. She loved and cared for them deeply. But she had been subtly infected with an unbiblical value system that said that to be worthwhile, she had to be superwoman. That meant having a superior education, having a career, and becoming the leader of, or at least being active in, many organizations and activities.

Initially in her marriage, Sally had tried to find satisfaction and significance by being a devoted wife and mother. To her dismay this didn't bring the desired results. In her disappointment, she began to add many new activities to her schedule and eventually took on leadership responsibilities. Sadly, though, what was supposed to bring relief added to her distress. She became bulimic, depressed, anxious, and frustrated. Eventually Sally became aware that she had been trying to find refreshment in "broken cisterns" that couldn't satisfy. She had been looking to people and things for meaning rather than to God. She had allowed her own opinions and the ideas of others to dominate her thinking.

God's Perspective

As Sally's attitude toward God changed, her attitude toward her family was altered as well. She decided to allow God to determine what really mattered in life. She saw from Scripture that God considers the family to be tremendously important. She chose to believe God's viewpoint on the place the family should have in her life.

Although Sally remained involved in some of her activities outside the home, she approached them with a different attitude and purpose. She was becoming a family-oriented person, serving rather than being served, and ministering out of the fullness of her relationship with God rather than to be fulfilled.

Christian wives and mothers are meant to be fruitful vines within their houses (Ps. 128:3). If you are a married woman, your family is to be your most outstanding ministry in life. The contribution you can make there to the kingdom of God and to society cannot be overestimated. Do not pay attention to anyone who denigrates the importance of the family. Your God says otherwise. Believe him!

Like the woman described in Proverbs 31, you may legitimately be involved in many things outside the home. Hopefully, you will use your God-given gifts to serve Christ and his people in your church and community. Perhaps you will give assistance to other Christian organizations. You may be legitimately employed in some occupation outside the home. But I encourage you to do whatever you do for the glory of God and for the sake of your family. Don't allow anything to interfere with those most important relationships.

The Need for Noble Character

In light of what we saw earlier about the basis for Christian conduct, it bears reemphasizing that the "fruitful vine" woman is a woman of "noble character" (Prov. 31:10, NIV). What she did was a *consequence* of her commitment to and relationship with God. Her deep reverence for God had produced within her a nobility of character, which then expressed itself in the exemplary attitudes and actions described in the passage. She is unselfish, generous, and caring. She is concerned for her family, for those who work for her, and for the poor and needy. She is disciplined. She can get up early in the morning or work into the night. She watches her diet and engages in enough physical activity to keep herself physically fit—her arms are strong.

She is contented and confident. She enjoys what she is doing. She can reflect on what she has done and sense that her gain is good. She is not so obsessed with her work that she doesn't have time to sit down and benefit from the fruits of her labors. She is able to put her arms around her children and listen to them. I suspect she is the kind of woman who even plays with them.

This woman knows how to smile and laugh. She is hopeful and positive in her outlook on the future. She is a fun person to be with. She can hang loose, work hard, and trust God. She likes people and wants to communicate with others in an encouraging way. She opens her mouth with wisdom, and the law of kindness is on her lips.

Some things in the passage suggest that this woman may not have been especially charming, radiant, or naturally beautiful. "Charm is deceitful and beauty is vain" (Prov. 31:30). Nevertheless she was beautiful in the most important sense—in her character and conduct. That made her a powerful influence in her home, among God's people, and in her world. She was a fruitful vine.

The Four Essential Factors

This woman points the way for all Christian married women. She had established four priorities in her life, and they are still relevant for women today: (1) her relationship with God, (2) her ministry to her family, (3) her development of godly character, and (4) her expression of godly conduct toward other people in and out of the home. Keep these four overlapping priorities in your life and you too will be a "fruitful vine" person. Your life will make an impact on your family, the church, and society.

Sally had to learn this, and by God's grace she did. May God in his grace help you to do the same.

Study and Application Assignments

Do the assignments individually and then discuss your answers with your mate or your study group.

1. Reflect on (or if necessary, review) this chapter and answer the following questions:

   a. Describe the problems in Sally's life and how they affected her and her family.

   b. How did she attempt to resolve these problems? How successful was she?

   c. How does Psalm 128 describe the wife and mother in God's kind of family?

   d. What does the vine simile suggest about the wife and mother? What does the word "fruitful" suggest about the woman's role and responsibility in the family?

   e. What does Genesis 2:18 teach about the woman's role in the family?

   f. What kinds of fruit will make the woman successful in her privilege and responsibility to build her family God's way?

   g. What is the first priority of the "fruitful vine" wife and mother? (See Prov. 31:30.)

   h. Why is this such a priority with the Proverbs 31 woman? How does this priority relate to her evident success?

   i. What is suggested by the fact that she is called a "woman of noble character"? (See Prov. 31:10 in the NASB.) What is character? Is this woman living life from the inside out or from the outside in?

   j. How does this woman's noble character manifest itself?

k. How (where) does this woman make her biggest contribution to God and society?

l. What kind of a relationship does she have with her husband and children? With people who work for her? With people outside the home?

m. What does Proverbs 31 indicate about a woman having a career outside the home?

n. What does Proverbs 31 say to make it clear that this woman was a fulfilled and fulfilling woman?

o. Think of two contemporary women who are fulfilled and fulfilling as the Proverbs 31 woman was. Do you find many of the same qualities in them as in her? What are their priorities? How are they like and unlike this woman?

p. What basic directives were given in chapter 2 about how to be a fulfilled and fulfilling woman?

q. Do you have any other biblical suggestions about how to be a "fruitful vine" woman?

r. How would you describe your relationship with God (your fear of God quotient)? (Excellent___, Good___, Vacillating___, Weak___, Very weak___, Nonexistent___.) Give reasons for your evaluation.

s. Evaluate yourself in terms of the teachings of this chapter. How do you fare in terms of being a "fruitful vine" woman—a woman of character, a woman who recognizes and fulfills the important role she has in her family, and a woman whose conduct generally reflects the conduct of the Proverbs 31 woman?

Allow for the differences in culture and situation, but use the basic principles. Don't assess on the basis of results; evaluate on the basis of your own life as compared to the priorities and characteristics described. You can't control results in your husband, children, or society.

With God's help, you can make progress in ordering your life according to the priorities mentioned in this chapter. By the power of the Holy Spirit, you can personally grow in the characteristics discussed. "As I look at my life, I see much___, some___, little___, no___ evidence that I am becoming a 'fruitful vine' woman." Explain your rating. (If you have difficulty answering this question, the "Fruitful Vine" Inventory found later in this assignment will help you.)

2. Study the following Bible verses about women, wives, mothers, fruit, and fruitbearing. Write down what they have to say and their application to your own life. Note what they suggest about the privileges, responsibilities, role, and value of women.

   a. Genesis 1:26-28

   b. Exodus 20:12

   c. Joshua 16:3-6

   d. 2 Kings 4:8-10

   e. Proverbs 1:8, 9

      6:20

      11:16

      12:4

      14:1

      18:22

      19:14

      20:20

      21:9, 19

      23:22-25

      31:10

      31:11, 12

      31:26

      31:28-31

   f. Ezekiel 24:16

   g. Matthew 26:13

      27:55-56

   h. Luke 1:30-38

      2:36-38

      8:3

      10:42

   i. John 15:1-16

      20:11-18

   j. Acts 1:14

    2:17, 18

    9:36-39

    16:14, 15

    21:9

  k. Romans 16:1, 2

    16:3

    16:6

    16:14, 15

  l. 1 Corinthians 7:2-5

  m. Ephesians 5:22-24, 33

  n. Philippians 4:3

  o. 1 Timothy 5:1, 2

    5:9-14

  p. 2 Timothy 1:5

    3:15

  q. Titus 3:2-5

  r. 1 Peter 3:1-6

3. Reflect on all you have just studied and try to record the most important overall impressions you have received about being a fulfilled and fulfilling woman. What broader, general principles did you find? List them.

  a.

  b.

  c.

  d.

  e.

  f.

  g.

  h.

4. Complete the following inventory. (Since this inventory was designed for wives and husbands, husbands would do well to use the same inventory.) Honest assessment should result in praise to God for whatever good he has worked in your life; confession to God and others

for sins that are revealed; renewed dedication to building your family God's way and to seeking God's help for changing those things that need to be changed.

FRUITFUL VINE OR WORTHY MATE INVENTORY

Based on Galatians 5:22, 23; 1 Peter 3:1-7; Proverbs 31:10-31; other Bible passages.

Read every statement carefully and then ask yourself, Is this true of me always (= 4), often (= 3), occasionally (= 2), seldom (= 1), or never (= 0)? Circle the number that honestly reflects what is true in your life. Don't overestimate or underestimate (Rom. 12:3). Make it a real learning experience.

1. I have a deep and meaningful relationship with God.	4 3 2 1 0
2. I am loving.	4 3 2 1 0
3. I am joyful.	4 3 2 1 0
4. I am peaceful.	4 3 2 1 0
5. I am peaceable.	4 3 2 1 0
6. I am gentle.	4 3 2 1 0
7. I am long-suffering, patient.	4 3 2 1 0
8. I am kind.	4 3 2 1 0
9. I am faithful, trustworthy, dependable.	4 3 2 1 0
10. I am self-controlled.	4 3 2 1 0
11. I am noble in character.	4 3 2 1 0
12. I am respected by my family.	4 3 2 1 0
13. I am devoted to my family.	4 3 2 1 0
14. I fulfill God-given family responsibilities.	4 3 2 1 0
15. I build up my family; I am an encourager.	4 3 2 1 0
16. I am devoted to ministering to others.	4 3 2 1 0
17. I am consistent and steadfast in doing right.	4 3 2 1 0
18. I am an industrious, hard-working person.	4 3 2 1 0
19. I am more concerned about character, proper attitudes, and right motives than I am about external beauty.	4 3 2 1 0
20. I am a fun person to be with.	4 3 2 1 0
21. I am not a workaholic. I can enjoy life, laugh, and relax.	4 3 2 1 0
22. I am basically contented and satisfied.	4 3 2 1 0
23. I am flexible and forbearing.	4 3 2 1 0
24. I am considerate of others.	4 3 2 1 0
25. I put others at ease.	4 3 2 1 0

26. I honor and respect others.	4 3 2 1 0
27. My speech is constructive and wholesome.	4 3 2 1 0
28. I exercise foresight and plan ahead.	4 3 2 1 0
29. I handle money wisely; I practice good stewardship.	4 3 2 1 0
30. I am willing to sacrifice for others.	4 3 2 1 0
31. I am orderly and organized.	4 3 2 1 0
32. I am not impulsive.	4 3 2 1 0
33. I am easily entreated.	4 3 2 1 0
34. I am sincere and honest.	4 3 2 1 0
35. I am a grateful person.	4 3 2 1 0
36. I am deeply committed to Jesus Christ.	4 3 2 1 0
37. I recognize that I constantly stand in need of God's mercy and grace.	4 3 2 1 0
38. I realize that any good thing found in me is the result of God's work in me.	4 3 2 1 0

5. What did you learn about yourself through this study? What are your strengths and weaknesses? What difference should all this make in your own life and family relationships?[1]

Notes

[1]Additional information with specific guidelines for the woman in the family is found in three books by Wayne Mack: *Strengthening Your Marriage, A Homework Manual for Biblical Living,* vol. 2, and *Preparing for Marriage God's Way.* A cassette tape focusing on being a fulfilled and fulfilling wife is available. These study materials may be secured from Biblical Counseling and Living Supplies, 2299 Brodhead Road, Bethlehem, Pa. 18017.

3

How to Grow Olive Plants—
Insights into Parent-Child Relations

If you were asked to describe parent-child relations in God's kind of family, what word picture would you use? Better still, what word picture do you think God would use?

We don't need to speculate on this matter. Psalm 128, the family song, provides God's description of parent-child relations in his kind of family: "Your children [shall be] like olive plants around your table" (Ps. 128:3). A commitment to the concepts embedded in these words will go a long way in helping your family to function effectively. Conversely, serious parent-child difficulties stem from misunderstanding or neglect of the truths captured by this phrase.

A House Divided

Harry and Mary Brown and their daughter Susan (pseudonyms) are living examples of what happens when the olive-plant concept is ignored. When they sought counseling, they were experiencing major family dysfunction.

At one time, all of them had professed faith in Christ. But fourteen-year-old Susan no longer called herself a Christian. "If being a Christian will make me like my mother, that's the last thing I want," she explained. Susan despised her mother and had no interest in the Christ she thought her mother represented. She avoided contact and communication with her mother as much as possible.

Susan's attitude toward her father, however, was much the

opposite. She normally showed him respect and love and shared freely what was going on in her life. She was willing to listen to him and took his suggestions seriously. Susan seemed to admire her father for the way he withstood abuse from her mother. At the same time, she pitied him for his unwillingness or inability to stand up to such mistreatment. "I don't know how or why he takes it," she would say.

As counseling progressed and more data was secured, it became evident that a father-daughter coalition had developed when Susan was very young. For years, Mary Brown was considered the common enemy (or at least an outsider) by both her husband and daughter. Harry looked to his daughter for "strokes" and sympathy. Susan depended on her father to protect her from her mother and to justify her attitudes and reactions toward her. Together they made quite a team.

As might be expected, this coalition between father and daughter proved a major source of frustration and antagonism to Mary. It appeared that Harry was more concerned about pleasing their daughter than about pleasing her. Mary was also convinced that Harry was too loose with Susan. "He's ruining her by his permissiveness," she complained. "He doesn't really know what's going on in her life."

All the data seemed to indicate that Susan was not an overtly "bad girl" in the popular sense. She was not into drugs or sexual immorality. In her dealings with people, she was not nasty, hardened, or resentful. With everyone except her mother, she was polite, respectful, and even somewhat cooperative. That was my experience with her as her counselor.

But Susan saw only two ways to resolve their family problems. Either she and her father could leave together, or she could leave alone. She was certain that she and her mother could never live peaceably in the same house.

Several times, in an attempt to relieve tensions, she had stayed for a few days with a friend without her parents' consent or knowledge. On at least two other occasions, Harry had arranged for her to stay with a Christian family until things cooled down at home. At times Harry himself would say: "I can't take it anymore.

Maybe the only solution is for me to take Susan and move away from Mary." And just as often, Mary would say: "If Harry doesn't change, I can't promise you what I might do. He'd better start being more of a leader or he may be sorry."

In the midst of all this, the Browns were all nice people in many ways. Individually, they were likable, honest, sincere, even generous. They attended church regularly and were involved in Bible study groups. They did what Christians are supposed to do.

Yet when it came to family relations, they had never paid much attention to what God had to say. On many family issues they simply did what came naturally rather than what comes biblically. Harry had his ideas of what was right for Susan, and Mary had hers. Unfortunately their ideas clashed. When they did study Scripture together, each would use the opportunity to prove his or her own point. Instead of coming to Scripture to be taught, reproved, corrected, and trained in righteousness (2 Tim. 3:16), they came looking for verses that would justify the positions they already held.

As a result, the Browns were a house divided, destroying each other by their selfishness. They would never be the blessed family of which Psalm 128 speaks until they were willing to bow humbly before God's Word as the standard for family living. They were failing as a family because neither Harry nor Mary had clearly understood or implemented a biblical view of parent-child relations, as depicted in the olive-plant concept. Let's make sure we don't make the same mistake.

Children as Part of God's Design

I think it's noteworthy that when God inspired the psalmist to write this family song, the family included children. To me, this seems to indicate that it is usually God's will for families to have children. This implication is explicitly taught or at least implied in other passages of Scripture. In Genesis, God gives clear teaching about this in his instructions to Adam and Eve. "Be fruitful and increase in number, fill the earth . . ." (Gen. 1:28, NIV).

In the last book of the Old Testament, Malachi challenges the casual view of marriage that people had in his day by reminding them that God ordained marriage. He goes on to say that one of the reasons for which God ordained marriage was so that godly offspring might be raised (Mal. 2:13-16, NIV).

New Testament teaching concurs with these Old Testament declarations. In one place, Paul says that he wants the younger widows to remarry and bear children (1 Tim. 5:14, NIV). In another place, he states that young women are to be encouraged (or taught) to love their husbands and their children (Titus 2:4). This statement assumes that most of the younger women will marry and will have children.

For all of these reasons, whenever couples say they don't want children, I commend them for their honesty, but also urge them to evaluate their reasons. When considering whether or not to have children, the Christian couple should ask, Lord, what do you want us to do? Scripture seems to indicate that unless there are good physical or spiritual reasons for not having children, God wants Christian couples to produce and raise godly offspring.

Having said that, I hasten to add that I do not believe that people should be coerced into conceiving children. People who are pushed into child-bearing are not likely to make good parents. The damage can be devastating.

It was to the Brown family. At the time of her marriage, Mary Brown was involved in a rewarding career. She enjoyed her work and was good at it. Besides this, the thought of parenthood with all its responsibilities left her feeling insecure and inadequate. The fact was that Mary really didn't want to have children.

Harry had different ideas. He asked, then begged, then tried to send Mary on a guilt trip. He used every means of persuasion he knew to get Mary to agree to have children. After a long time of this, Mary reluctantly conceded. Soon, Susan was conceived. Mary was pregnant but she didn't like it. She resented Harry and eventually her daughter for the way her life had to change. On top of that, she experienced guilt because she knew that her attitude toward Susan and Harry was sinful.

Mary was between a rock and a hard place. She knew she should deal with her sinful resentment, but she didn't really want to give it up, because it was her way of punishing Harry for what he had done to her. Unwilling to grant Harry complete forgiveness, she chose to hang on to her resentment. Mary had the child, but only because she was forced into it. And that laid the groundwork for the family's tremendous problems.

Reasons to Be a Parent

Mary and Harry were both wrong in their approach to having children. Her main concern was not what God wanted, but what she wanted. His main concern was not God's desires, but his own aspirations. And he was determined to see his desire fulfilled even if he had to manipulate Mary until she gave superficial consent. She may have acquiesced on the outside, but she was rebelling on the inside. Her life is a tragic illustration of the fact that people should not be coerced into parenting.

Those who have unbiblical reasons for not wanting children need to deal with the root of their problem. With honesty they should identify and resolve the unbiblical reasons for their aversion. Sinful heart issues must be faced and resolved. Christ's forgiveness and help for internal change must be sought. God's perspective on children must be understood and believed.

As I write these words, I'm aware that some of you may be very godly people who do not have children, perhaps for some very good, spiritual, God-honoring reasons. Perhaps you have been gifted and called to a particular kind of ministry that would preclude fulfilling the responsibilities of biblical parenting. Possibly, you are temporarily in a situation that would make it very difficult on the children. It could be that you are postponing parenthood until certain personal or interpersonal problems are cleared up. What's best for the children and for the kingdom of God are the major factors in your decision on whether and when to have children.

It may also be that some of you are physically unable to have children. You want to, but you can't. Please don't allow yourself to descend into despair by focusing on what cannot be. Rather, seek God's help to avail yourself of the opportunities you do have to nurture children in godly ways in your larger family—the church (Mark 3:35; 1 Tim. 5:1, 2). Ask God to show you how and with whom you can do your part in raising godly offspring for him.

Parenting Is a Privilege

There's a sense in which every Christian couple can have children. All married Christians may and should be involved in some kind of parenting. And that's exciting, because according to the family song (Ps. 128), parenting is a privilege. The statement about children in the family song (Ps. 128:3) is followed by an exclamation concerning the blessedness of parenting (Ps. 128:4). In a similar vein, a previous psalm asserts that "children are a gift from the Lord" and that the person whose quiver is full of them is a blessed individual (Ps. 127:3-5).

By giving you children, almighty God has given to you one of the most important, exalted, rewarding, challenging opportunities that you could ever have. He is calling you to help in growing a human being for him. He has commissioned you to labor with him in building a life through which he may be glorified and great good may be accomplished for other people.

As a parent, yours is the challenge of bringing a person up to be a fruitful disciple of Jesus Christ. In the words of Psalm 128, you can play a major role in growing children who are like luxurious, prolific olive plants.

Mary and Harry Brown needed this perspective on parenting. Their vision was too limited, their attitude ungodly. They failed to perceive how their lives and relationship were impacting negatively on another human being. Both of them lacked the big picture of what God's way of parenting involves in terms of its privileges, responsibilities, and methods. Both of them were too selfish, too nearsighted, too man-centered in their parental endeavors. Neither of them had a clear understanding of the implications of the olive-plant picture that God uses to describe parent-child relations in Psalm 128.

Children as Olive Plants

What exactly does the olive-plant picture mean? What does it suggest about parent-child relations? How can an understanding of this simile help you to avoid the mistakes Harry and Mary Brown made?

For one thing, the psalmist's simile implies that you should have a high regard for your children. One author tells us that the olive tree was the most important tree in Palestine.[1] In one passage of Scripture, the olive tree is depicted as the king of the trees (Judg. 9:8, 9). Another reference dignifies it by comparing God's people to an olive tree planted by God (Rom. 11:17ff.). Other portions of Scripture exalt this tree by specifically prescribing that the oil of the olive tree—and only that oil—be used to consecrate the priests and fuel the lamps in the tabernacle (Exod. 27:20; 30:22-33). In other words, the psalmist was describing children in a way that emphasized how valuable and precious they were.

Jesus felt the same way. He knew all about children. He knew that they were born sinners and therefore needed to be regenerated and redeemed (Pss. 51:3-5; 58:3). He was fully aware that they needed to be changed by God's grace (Eph. 2:1-8). He had no unrealistic ideas about their perfection or innocence (Prov. 22:15). Yet he evidenced a high regard for them. At times, he used them as illustrations of spiritual truth (Matt. 18:1-10). He emphasized the seriousness of mistreating them. He sternly rebuked his disciples for trying to prevent certain parents from bringing their children to him (Mark 10:13, 14). Calmly yet forcefully he said: "Let the little children come to me, and do not hinder them.... I tell you the truth, anyone who will not receive the kingdom of God like a little child will never enter it." Having done that, "he took the children in his arms, put his hands on them and blessed them" (Mark 10:14-16).

Like Jesus, you must be realistic in your attitude toward your children. You must realize that your children have the potential for great wickedness (Pss. 51:5; 58:3). They are born sinners and must be regenerated by God's Spirit and redeemed by God's grace. Your children need God's forgiveness for their sins. They need his help to become truly worthwhile, God-honoring, olive-plant persons. Without him, they cannot bear fruit for God (John 15:1-6).

However, viewing your children biblically has another side to it as well. Biblical realism also requires you to see your children as persons of great value and worth, despite their needs and deficiencies. What this means is that your children should be important to you not primarily because they are yours, but because they are persons made in God's image and are God's gifts to you.

Let your thinking be gripped by the realization that each of your children is destined to live forever. Recall that he or she has the potential to do immense good—or evil. Understand that by God's grace your child has great potential to become a thriving olive plant according to Psalm 128.

A "Plant" of Great Potential

In doing research on the olive plant, I was interested to note the numerous ways in which the olive plant and its fruit were used. Olives and olive oil were used for food (Deut. 24:20), illumination (Lev. 24:2), consecrating religious workers (Exod. 30:22-33), cosmetic purposes (Ruth 3:3), medicinal and hygienic functions (Luke 10:34), religious ceremonies (Gen. 28:18), and even as a commodity of exchange (1 Kings 5:11; Luke 16:6).

In addition, the olive tree and its fruit are symbols of joy, prosperity, and peace (Isa. 61:3; Ps. 45:7). The tree itself was noted for its beauty (Jer. 11:16; Hos. 14:6). Its wood was valuable for fuel and construction purposes (1 Kings 6:23, 31-33). When the olive crop failed, it was considered a national tragedy (Hab. 3:17).

What does all of this indicate about the way you should regard your children? It suggests that you should have high expectations for them. Make sure your expectations are in keeping with their personal gifting and stage of development, but don't underestimate their God-given capacities. Encourage them to believe that, in keeping with their gifting and maturity level, they can make important contributions even now.

To be sure, olive plants need careful attention to bear fruit. The soil around them must frequently be plowed. They need water and fertilizer. They thrive best in warm and sunny situations.[2]

Learn from this the importance of giving your children diligent care. Do your utmost to bring them up in the instruction and discipline of the Lord (Eph. 6:4). Be diligent in teaching them God's Word in structured and spontaneous situations. Be genuinely and attractively spiritual in your lifestyle. Hide God's Word in your own heart. Make your entire life a living epistle to your children of

God's truth. Provide an environment that is conducive to the development of godly character and conduct. Make yourself and your home a fun place to be. Seek to eliminate from yourself and your home anything that would inhibit fruitfulness.

At the same time, don't try to bear fruit *for* your children. The olive tree must bear its own fruit. Teach them to accept that responsibility. Don't be guilty of excessive pushing or shoving. Exude realistic optimism. Develop the hopeful and appropriate expectation that they will be productive.

Plants, Not Branches

I'm intrigued that the family song states that our children are to be like olive plants, not branches (Ps. 128:3). A plant has an independent existence. A branch is simply a part of the tree. This points to the fact that we are to respect the individuality of our children. God didn't intend for them to be carbon copies of us. Let your children have ideas different from your own. Don't be threatened by differences of opinion. Rather, help your children to think through issues for themselves. Of course, you are to stand firmly, calmly, and intelligently on issues where you have a "thus saith the Lord." However, beware of getting involved in unnecessary power struggles. Don't create issues where there's no need to. Within the perimeters of Scripture, give your children freedom to be themselves.

In your parenting, provide fences, not straitjackets. Establish biblical limits and then train your children to obey them. In their earliest years the fences will need to be much more restrictive and clearly delineated. You will be more involved in decision making, in determining specific policies, in helping your children to fulfill certain responsibilities, in discerning what is right and wrong. But even in these earliest years, make sure that you give your children room to maneuver for themselves. Restrain yourself from doing for them what they can and should do for themselves. Provide the tools, the encouragement, the example, and the structure for them to produce their own fruit.

As they mature, the fences can be expanded so that your children assume more and more responsibility for their own lives.

What you want to develop is inner motivation and self-control—
the ability to think, choose, and live biblically without the need for
excessive external motivation or control.

Your goal is to help your child grow up to be "interdependently
dependent" on Christ and his Word. You want them to be plants
within a larger olive orchard—that's the interdependent part. They'll
need to relate to other people, in a giving and receiving relationship.
Unlike lone olive trees isolated out in the desert, they are to be like
olive plants around your table, associated with you and in some
ways open to helping you, as well as receiving your help.

Having said that, the fact remains that your children are to be
plants not branches. Ultimately, you should want to point them
away from yourself to Christ as the one upon whom they are most
dependent. You'll want them to experience the freedom for which
Christ has set them free. You'll desire them to have a mature
relationship, not a dependency relationship, with you. You'll believe
that by God's grace, your children can and must bear fruit on their
own.

An Unbalanced Perspective

The Brown family was far from this ideal. Neither parent
showed a high regard for Susan. Mary was unbalanced in the way
she focused mainly on Susan's negative qualities. Harry was apparently blind to Susan's potential for evil. He could find an
excuse for almost anything she did. This hindered his relationship
with Mary. She saw it as a personal rejection of her perspective and
an unwillingness to provide the discipline Susan really needed.
Harry's apparent blind spots were also a detriment to Susan. You
don't correct one imbalance by creating another. Susan was not
learning from either parent how to evaluate herself accurately. Nor
was she being taught to take responsibility for her own attitudes
and responses. She was not being encouraged to handle problems
and sins in a biblical way.

On the surface Harry appeared to respect Susan. But by not
encouraging her to think biblically about herself or others, he was
actually showing low expectations of her. The truth was that if

Harry and Mary wanted to help Susan grow God's way, they both needed to adopt a more biblical, realistic, balanced view of their daughter.

It's Up to You

A key teaching of Psalm 128:3 is that your children are to be like olive plants around *your* table. Before God, *you*, and not the state or the school or even the church, are responsible for providing for your children (Ps. 23:4; 1 Tim. 5:8). *You* are to nurture them for God.

This nurturing includes their physical, mental, social, emotional, and spiritual needs. You may employ the help of others in fulfilling these needs, but in the final analysis, God says the buck stops with you. You must either provide for your children personally or secure assistance in doing so. Either way, you must supervise the process and do your utmost to see that your children's needs are adequately met.

All of this assumes that you will spend quality time with your children. After all, their being around *your* table implies that you are there as well. You can't know the needs of your children unless you give them your focused attention. You've got to study them, listen to them, talk to them, play with them, think about them, and pray over them if you're going to know what provision they need from your table.

This picture of your children like olive plants around your table conveys the idea of fellowship and loyalty. It suggests that building your family God's way involves developing family cohesiveness and togetherness.

Unfortunately, this kind of togetherness or family spirit does not just happen. You can't wish it into existence. It must be cultivated. But how? I would like to offer some suggestions. You can foster a spirit of loyalty and togetherness in your family by:

1. Making Christ the focal point of your family relations. Commitment to Christ should bind the family not only to Christ, but to each other.

2. Communicating realistic optimism and expectancy for every person. Don't express by word or action that you have given up on

any family member, or that you are resigning him or her to failure.

3. Valuing the opinion of every family member and giving all family members time to express themselves and their ideas. Allow for a free exchange of thoughts without condemnation or ridicule.

4. Projecting the positive feeling that all family members complement and complete one another.

5. Building a museum of positive family memories. Play games with your children. Involve them in your activities. Enjoy each child individually. Keep a memory box for each child. Develop family traditions. Take advantage of prime times. Do the unusual with your children. Make big deals of special occasions. Make special occasions when there are no special occasions. Let different members plan vacations or other events.

6. Developing family pride. Talk about the strengths and accomplishments of various family members.

7. Becoming authentically like Christ and displaying in your life the fruit of the Spirit. It's hard not to respect and be attracted to someone of whom this is true.

8. Determining fair family discipline guidelines.

9. Not joking or jesting at the expense of any family member.

10. Discussing adequately major changes in family rules, decisions and activities.

11. Avoiding physical or psychological child abuse.

12. Becoming interested in the interests of each family member.

13. Avoiding being overly permissive or overly strict in your discipline.

14. Including family members in family planning.

15. Giving each family member freedom to make decisions wherever you can legitimately do so.

16. Being biblically realistic in your expectations of each family member.

17. Freely expressing your love for every family member by word and deed.

18. Being more concerned about Christian attitudes and character than you are about performance or other externals.

19. Administering discipline fairly and consistently.

20. Looking upon every family member as a "human becoming" as well as a human being. We are all in process. None of us has arrived at perfection yet.

21. Being very sensitive to the needs, feelings, and fears of every family member.

22. Avoiding the use of angry or exasperated words.

23. Making it easy for every family member to approach you with problems and concerns.

24. Making your home a center of Christian hospitality where your children are brought into frequent contact with vibrant Christians.

25. Developing family projects that involve every family member.

26. Learning how to face family problems and not ignore them.

27. Forgiving the sins and failures—past and present—of family members.

28. Supporting one another through failures.

29. Correlating schedules to have time together. Schedule regular family times and time for each individual.

30. Asking forgiveness when you wrong one another.

31. Appropriate touching and hugging.

32. Clarifying the basic responsibilities of family members.

33. Refusing to use fear or guilt as a means of bringing others into conformity.

34. Expressing confidence in one another.

35. Making the Bible, not your own opinions, the standard for personal and family living.

36. Maintaining a deep, personal relationship with Jesus Christ. Jesus Christ in you will draw you to each other.

37. Becoming involved in Christian activities as a family.

38. Worshipping God as a family in your home and in the church.

39. Praying regularly for every family member individually and for your family as a whole.

Following these guidelines will create an environment that will help you to build your family God's way. They will help your children to be like olive plants around your table.[3]

Study and Application Assignments

Do the assignments individually and then discuss your answers with your mate or your study group.

1. Reflect on (or if necessary, review) this chapter and answer the following questions:

   a. What word picture of parent-child relations does God use in Psalm 128:3?

   b. What does the Bible teach about whether or not married people should have children? Support your answer with Scripture.

   c. What are some reasons people give for not having children?

   d. Are there legitimate reasons for a couple not having children? If so, what are they?

   e. What happened in the Brown family when Mary Brown was coerced into having children?

   f. What was meant by the statement that there is a sense in which "every Christian couple can have children"? How can you appropriately help others to raise their children? How can (and do) others help you?

   g. What does the fact that children are compared to *olive* plants (not weeds or bramble bushes) indicate about the way we should regard our children?

   h. Why is a person's attitude toward children so important in the question of having and raising children?

   i. How does the Lord Jesus Christ illustrate by his example or teachings the high regard that he had for children?

   j. What are two extremes we must avoid when viewing our children?

   k. What does the fact that children are compared to olive *plants* (not trees) indicate about the needs of children? What do olive plants need from their caretakers? What do children need from their parents?

   l. What does the fact that children are compared to olive *plants* (not olive branches) suggest about parent-child relations?

   m. How do parents sometimes violate the olive-plant concept of parent-child relations? What two mistakes do parents often make? Think of illustrations in the Bible or in your own experience (personal or by observation) of when and how this concept has been disobeyed.

Identify how this violation has affected the children.

n. What two concepts do the words "around your table" denote about building your family God's way?

2. Meditate on the thirty-nine suggestions for building your family God's way included at the end of the teaching section of this chapter. Consider what each of them means in practical, behavioral terms. Take each statement and use the following rating scale to evaluate your parenting quotient for each of your children: regularly (= 4), often (= 3), occasionally (= 2), seldom (= 1), never (= 0). After you have rated yourself on each of the thirty-nine statements, make a list of all the items that you scored 0 or 1 or 2. Plan what and how you can improve in these areas. Discuss these items with your mate. Perhaps you will want to write out a statement of commitment and sign your name to what you are going to do. Pray daily for God's help in making the desired improvements. Refer back to your list regularly as a reminder and a means of continuous evaluation and motivation.

3. Study the following Bible verses on parent-child relations. Write down what each passage teaches or implies about parenting. Try to gain specific insights about what you are doing or should do to build your family God's way. As you look at each passage ask yourself: What is God saying to me about parenting? How should it be applied in my family? How well am I doing in implementing the teaching(s) of this passage in my parenting efforts?

a. Proverbs 1:8, 9

b. Proverbs 4:1, 2

c. Proverbs 5:7-23

d. Proverbs 6:1-35

e. Proverbs 7:1-27

f. Proverbs 10:1, 5

g. Proverbs 13:1

h. Proverbs 13:24

i. Proverbs 14:1

j. Proverbs 15:27

k. Proverbs 19:18

l. Proverbs 22:6

    m. Proverbs 22:15

    n. Proverbs 23:13

    o. Proverbs 23:15, 16

    p. Proverbs 23:24

    q. Proverbs 27:8

    r. Proverbs 29:15

    s. Proverbs 29:17

    t. Proverbs 31:15

       31:21

       31:27

       31:28

    u. Deuteronomy 6:4-9

    v. Ephesians 6:4; Colossians 3:21

    w. 2 Corinthians 12:15

    x. 1 Thessalonians 2:7, 8, 11

    y. 1 Timothy 3:4, 5

    z. 2 Timothy 1:5; 3:15

4. Individually answer the following questions. Be specific in your answers; give details. Then discuss them with your mate. Use this inventory to affirm your positives and discover and change your negatives in parenting.

    a. When you instruct your child to do something, what do you do if he disobeys? Do you do the same thing with each child and every time?

    b. What do you do if a child resorts to tantrums, pouts, screams, mumbles under his breath, becomes abusive, walks out, pounds walls, or kicks? Do you react the same way with each child?

    c. When you ask one of your children to do something, how often do you ask? Are you consistent in the way you respond?

    d. When a child has a hard time fulfilling assignments and responsibilities, what do you do? Do you react the same way with each child?

    e. How is each child like or unlike you in his personality, attitudes, values, relationships, goals, actions, reactions, speech, interests, ways of handling situations?

f. Do you and your mate agree on what you expect of each child (chores, responsibilities, behavior, manners, etc.)? On the way you discipline and why? (Note any areas of disagreement.)

g. What do you do that communicates love, appreciation, respect, concern, devotion, trust, and understanding to each child? What do you do to help each child know he is special?

h. What do you do that may be (or at least may be perceived by the child as) disrespectful, unloving, disloyal, selfish, unconcerned, or stubborn to each child?

i. Reflect on your relationship with each child and note the high and low points and why they were that way. (I.e.,what made them high or low points? What was happening at the time?)

j. What are the abilities, qualities, assets, and interests of each child? How do you encourage them to develop these features?

k. What are the weaknesses, problems, and un-Christlike features of each child? What has been your response to them?

l. What do you do that makes it easy for each child to open up with you, to respect you and think of you as someone who is approachable and nice to be with? What do you do that may foster the opposite attitudes?

m. Think of the best parents you know, and write down everything you observe as strengths in them and their relationship with their children.

n. If you were to describe your family life with one word, what would the word be?

o. Write down your goals for your family life.

p. Write down what you think your children would say about your family.

q. Finish these sentences:

Parents are . . .

A good rule in our home is . . .

A rule in our home that I'd like to change is . . .

Our family relations would be better if . . .

I wish our family would . . .

In our family, God is . . .

Notes
   [1]Winifred Walker, *All the Plants of the Bible* (Garden City, N.Y.: Doubleday, 1979), p. 154.
   [2]E. W. G. Masterman, "Olive Tree," in *The International Standard Bible Encyclopaedia*, ed. James Orr, 5 vols. (Wilmington, Del.: Associated Publishers and Authors, n.d.), 4:2184.
   [3]Additional information about the specifics of biblical parenting is found in the books *Strengthening Your Marriage*, pp. 113-48 and *A Homework Manual for Biblical Living*, vol. 2, pp. 71-90. Several tapes entitled, *God's Plan for Rearing Children* (3 tapes), *Effective Mothering, Effective Fathering, What to Do When Your Children Rebel*, and *Counseling Adolescents* (4 tapes) are also available. These study materials may be secured from Biblical Counseling and Living Supplies, 2299 Brodhead Road, Bethlehem, Pa. 18017.

PART TWO

DEVELOPING GOD-HONORING FAMILY RELATIONSHIPS

4

I Heard What You Didn't Say

Some time ago I was a guest on a radio talk program. A caller asked me, "What do you think is the biggest hindrance to marital and family unity today?" That's a difficult question, but I answered that one of the biggest hindrances to marital and family happiness is poor communication. As a counselor I frequently encounter people who cannot resolve their problems or develop deep relationships because they don't know how to communicate effectively.

Without good communication you can't have the kind of marriage or family God wants you to have. As Jay Adams points out in his book *Christian Living in the Home,* when it comes to interpersonal relationships, communication comes *first.* It is a primary need. For that reason I want to devote the next several chapters to a discussion of what constitutes effective communication and how it may be developed. I hope you will be encouraged to evaluate your own communication with your family and with others outside the home.

What Is Effective Communication?

Generally, effective communication may be defined as the process of sharing information with another person in such a way that the sender's message is understood as he intended it. Unless the sender and receiver have come to a common meaning, they haven't communicated effectively. In Ephesians 4 Paul says that we are to speak what is good for edification according to the need of the moment, that we may minister grace or help to our hearers (v. 29).

That powerful chapter of Scripture indicates that when people have communicated effectively, they are mutually strengthened, encouraged, and enriched.

That is the standard by which we must evaluate our marital and family communication. Does it foster harmony, unity, and emotional closeness? Does it draw people together? Do we experience not just physical closeness but emotional closeness? Is our experience like that of David and Jonathan, whose souls were knit together in an emotional bond of brotherly love (1 Sam. 18:1)?

That is what effective communication does. And that is why it is so tremendously important in marriage and family relationships. In many families, people may live together physically but are emotionally miles apart. They can hardly imagine the kind of harmony in which their hearts beat together. Such a comprehensive unity and deep intimacy escapes them because they are not communicating effectively.

Wherever you find people fulfilling the "one flesh" concept that God intends for married people (Gen. 2:24), you will find people who communicate effectively. That is because the one-flesh principle involves more than physical union. It implies emotional closeness, harmony, and intimacy, which are the inevitable outgrowth of effective communication.

Nonverbal Communication

I've entitled this chapter "I Heard What You Didn't Say" to call attention to a much-overlooked aspect of communication: the nonverbal element. It's important to recognize that communication is more than words. It also involves accurately sending and receiving the right kind of nonverbal messages.

Many examples of nonverbal communication appear in Scripture. At the time of their creation, we're told that Adam and Eve were both naked and not ashamed (Gen. 2:25). That said something about their relationship with each other and with God. They had no shame or embarrassment because there was no guilt. Their consciences were clear. Because their hearts were pure and holy, they felt comfortable with each other and with God.

Later, when they had disobeyed God's command by eating from the tree of the knowledge of good and evil (Gen. 2:17; 3:6), their nonverbal behavior expressed clearly that something had changed. They tried to cover up (Gen. 3:7), and when God came walking in the garden in the cool of the day (Gen. 3:8), they did something that they had never done before. They hid. Without saying a word Adam and Eve declared that something was seriously wrong. They didn't have to explain, "We ate of the forbidden fruit, and now we're ashamed." Their actions said it all.

Another example of the power of nonverbal communication is found in a later chapter of Genesis. Scripture tells us that the sons of Jacob knew that he loved Joseph more than them (Gen. 37:3, 4). We know this because the Bible explicitly states it. But Joseph's brothers knew it from what they saw, rather than from what they heard or read (Gen. 37:4). I doubt that Jacob went around saying: "Joseph is my favorite son. I love him much more than the rest of you." But the fact was that he did love Joseph more than all the others, and his nonverbal behavior conveyed that message forcefully.

Jacob's sons heard what he didn't say. And the same thing happens today. Others hear what we're not saying because we're constantly sending out messages without even opening our mouths. The truth is that we are never not communicating, even when we are silent.

Common Forms of Silent Communication

With our eyes we communicate with one another by the way we look or don't look at each other. If I avoid eye contact with you, I'm communicating. If I roll my eyes when you're talking to me, you get a particular message. We communicate with our facial expressions, whether a stern look or pleasant. My frowns, my smiles, my smirks, my pouts, my worried or angry or fearful facial expressions all convey a message to you.

We also communicate by the way we dress. Our clothing reveals whether we are sloppy or neat, whether we are organized, whether we care about clothes. We often indicate what we think about others by the way we dress around them. When husbands or wives refuse to wear what their spouses want them to wear, a message is being sent. A person doesn't have to say, "I don't like you," or "I don't care what you think" to convey that message in a nonverbal way .

We may communicate by the way we sit or stand. If when you walk up to some people, they back off, they may be telling you that you're invading their private space. Perhaps they don't know you or trust you sufficiently to let you get that close to them. They may be announcing that you can't crash your way into their lives. If someone turns his back to you, the message may even be stronger.

I usually watch how people sit when they come into my counseling office. Some of them pull their chairs up as close to the desk as they can. Others push their chairs away. When some families come in, the wife always sits to the right, and the husband to the left. Their child inevitably takes the middle chair, positioning himself as close to the mother and as far from the father as possible. With other families, after Mom and Dad seat themselves beside each other on one side of the room, the child opts for the other side.

An astute observer will glean from these arrangements much information about family coalitions and interactions. For example, the first child may have aligned himself more closely with Mom, considering her to be his ally and protector. The second child may consider himself an outsider, not especially close to either Mom or Dad.

People also communicate by their use of time. Show me how you use your time and I'll know a lot about your values. If you tell me that your relationship with God is the most important factor in your life, and yet you don't have time for church or prayer or Bible study, your actions speak more loudly than your words. If you say your family is important to you, but you don't have time to spend with them, I'll know your family is not important enough to you.

We also communicate by the way we use our money. If we spend our money on all kinds of things, but don't give to the Lord's work or to needy people, we declare where our treasure is, and what our values are. Jesus indicates that the way we use our money is a trustworthy barometer of our character and our reliability. In fact, he says that if a person is faithful to God in the stewardship of his material possessions (an area he describes as "a little thing"), he can be trusted to be faithful in other areas as well. But if a person can't be trusted in the economic realm, he can't be trusted in any other realm either (Luke 16:11, 12).

The way we laugh and what we laugh at say much about our attitudes and values. We communicate by our willingness to help others and by the spirit or manner in which we help. Without our speaking a word, people get the message either that we are glad to give assistance or that we are doing it grudgingly because we don't know how to get out of it.

We communicate with our ears—by whether we are willing to listen to people. As I look over my classes, I sometimes see students leaning forward, literally doing what Proverbs says. They are inclining their ears to hear what is being said. The nonverbal behavior of others suggests that they are inclining their ears *not* to hear. Without saying a word, these students express their different levels of interest.

We also communicate with our arms and our hands. When I put my arms around my wife, I'm sending a message to her. Even our absence or presence indicates whether we are willing or unwilling to spend time with somebody.

The Power of Nonverbal Communication

It could be argued that we do more communicating nonverbally than verbally. And since communication involves everything we do as well as say, we are communicating all the time. Even our attempts to avoid communication send their own kind of message. The question is not Will we or won't we communicate? but Are we communicating effectively? That question can't be answered affirmatively unless we are sending and receiving the right kind of nonverbal messages.

Nonverbal messages are powerful. God's nonverbal communication to us through the cross is the most powerful communication you could imagine. How could God say "I love you" more powerfully then he did through the giving of his own Son for us?

Indeed, after reminding us that God did not spare his own Son but delivered him up for us all, Paul goes on to ask, "How will He not also with Him freely give us all things?" (Rom. 8:32). God has unmistakably and irrefutably asserted his infinite love for us through the powerful nonverbal message of the cross.

In the midst of a powerful passage on church unity, Paul says to the Ephesians, "Let him who steals steal no longer; but rather let him labor, performing with his own hands what is good, in order that he may have something to share with him who has need" (4:28). Why does Paul bring up stealing in a passage about interpersonal relationships? The point is this: if we say that we really care for people and yet steal from them, our actions contradict our words. Stealing from people and loving them don't go together. If you really want to get along with people, Paul explains, you must stop stealing and start working and giving. In other words, demonstrate your concern for others by ministering in practical ways to their needs. Stop thinking only about yourself, and what others can do for you. Practice thinking and acting like their needs are important to you. Such actions speak volumes of your love for others.

Create Your Own Environment

Never underestimate the significance of your nonverbal behavior. Nothing is more significant in our relationships with other people. In a very real sense, we can create our own environments by influencing how others respond to us, positively or negatively.

Recently a young man who had gotten into some serious trouble was sharing with me some things that bothered him. In particular he didn't like the way his mother treated him. "She's constantly telling me to be home at a certain time. She's afraid I'll be kidnapped. She wants to know where I'm going, what I do, who I'm with, when I'll be back. Here I am, sixteen years old, and she's treating me like a little baby, constantly checking up on me."

I asked him, "Do you have any idea why your mom does this and would you like some help in getting your mom off your back?"

He responded: "No, I don't know why she does this. And yes, I'd like help in getting her to treat me more like an adult."

"Do you think there is any possibility that you taught your mom to treat you this way?" I asked.

With a puzzled expression he replied, "What do you mean?"

I answered, "Let me illustrate with an example. Some time ago one of our sons worked in a take-out seafood restaurant. Before long the owner developed a high regard for Chip and made him assistant manager. Chip's boss had such confidence in him that he would often put him in charge and not even come into the restaurant. The owner frequently told us how much he appreciated Chip, and how he wished he could find other workers like him. Recently, we saw this man again. Our son had not worked for him for more than two years, but he lamented that he still had not found anyone to replace Chip. Said the owner, 'People like him are hard to find.' "

At that point I said to the young man I was counseling, "Do you know why this restaurant owner had such a high opinion of our son and wanted other employees like him?"

"Well, I guess he trusted him."

"How do you think he came to believe that he could trust my son?"

"I guess he saw what your son was doing and figured that he was trustworthy."

"And how did he get that idea? Who taught him to view Chip that way?"

"I guess Chip did."

"So, what you're saying is that my son helped to create his own environment. Because of his reliability, he taught this man that he could be trusted. Now, suppose Chip had always come in fifteen minutes late or cheated on his time card or loafed on the job? Suppose he had refused to follow the boss's instructions or sneaked a free meal to one of his friends. What do you think the boss would have done then?"

"He probably would have fired him—or at least would have watched him more. I guess he'd push him a little harder and wonder if he could be trusted."

"Right! My son would have taught him that he could not be trusted. Again, my son would have created his own environment by influencing the way this man acted toward him. Now, how might all this apply to what's happening with your mother? What does this suggest about how you can get your mother to treat you more like an adult?"

"I guess if I want her to treat me like an adult, I have to act more like an adult. I have to be more open with her and teach her I can be trusted."

From there, we went on to discuss how he could teach his mother to treat him differently. We reflected on what he was doing to reinforce her tendency to treat him like a child. We considered what he could do to communicate to his mother that he was trustworthy. We explored the biblical concept that we often reap what we sow (only more so) and decided how and what to sow differently.

The lesson here is that our actions tend to create reactions in our environment, including the home. And our reactions to others encourage certain responses on their part, whether good or bad. Before we complain about the behavior of other family members, we need to consider how we are provoking them or responding to them. The scriptural admonition not to return evil for evil, or insult for insult, but rather to give a blessing (1 Pet. 3:9), recognizes the domino and boomerang effects of much behavior. Our behavior may actually trigger or reinforce in others the kinds of behavior we oppose, whether grumpiness, distrust, condemnation, or strife.

Misunderstood Messages

Sadly, nonverbal communication is often misunderstood, even when God is sending the message. Through creation God is constantly declaring his glory, but how many of us see it? People either ignore the message about God proclaimed through God's world or else they see in creation what they consider to be evidences of evolution. They completely misunderstand the message God is sending.

People also misinterpret God's revelation clearly displayed in providence. Scripture teaches that history is *his story,* but very few acknowledge God's hand in the affairs of men. Even Christians sometimes misunderstand God's nonverbal behavior. Hebrews

12:6 states that God's chastening or discipline is an evidence of his love for us. It proves that he is our father and we are members of his family. But there are many times that we don't see it that way. That is why the Bible says, "Don't faint or become weary when you are chastened by him" (Heb. 12:5). We don't always recognize that what happens to us is a reflection of God's love for us.

In like fashion, the nonverbal behavior of men is often misconstrued by others. Do you remember the Old Testament case in which Eli misinterpreted Hannah's behavior when he came into the temple and saw her there (1 Sam. 1:12-18). The Bible tells us that she was distressed because she wanted a child. As she earnestly prayed to God in deep and sincere faith, Eli observed that her lips were moving though she made no sound. Thinking Hannah was drunk, he sternly rebuked her for her intemperance. Eli had completely misinterpreted her nonverbal behavior.

The New Testament describes a similar event in the book of Acts. On the day of Pentecost, when the Spirit of God powerfully came upon the Christians in Jerusalem, they took to the streets, speaking in other languages, witnessing, and preaching about Jesus. Some people noticed the way these Christians were behaving and concluded that they were drunk (Acts 2:1-15).

The actions of these Christians were grossly misunderstood. And if it happened then, it can happen today. People will be prone to misconstrue our nonverbal behavior. While assuming that they hear what we're not saying, they may draw the wrong conclusions. And that will influence the way they think, act, and feel about us, inaccurate or not.

We must realize too that *we* may misread the nonverbal communication of others. It's one thing to grant that others err in understanding our actions. But for some reason we are reluctant to take seriously our own potential for misjudging the actions of others. All too often, we quickly and dogmatically assume that we have accurately heard what the other person didn't say. For example, we might not think to question our interpretation of why another family member did something and what he meant by it. We're sure we have it figured out. How could we be wrong! Others have been wrong about us, but, in our pride, we seldom consider that we could be just as wrong about them. Though sad experience has proved us in error a thousand other times, we convince ourselves that this time we are right. And so we act and react accordingly.

In an article entitled "How We Send Emotional Messages," Ernst Beier graphically illustrates how easily we can mistake the messages people are conveying nonverbally.

> We asked several people to act out six different moods on video-tape. The moods were anger, fear, seductivity, indifference, happiness and sadness. Then we let our subjects review their portrayals and eliminate any that they felt were unrepresentative. . . .
>
> When we played these videotapes to large audiences to discover if they could decode the moods intended, we found that . . . everyone appears to send out misinformation. . . .
>
> I shall never forget two examples of this discordance. One girl, who tried like everyone else to appear angry, fearful, seductive, indifferent, happy and sad . . . appeared to her judges as angry in every case. Imagine what a difficult world she must have lived in. No matter where she set the thermostat of her emotional climate, everyone else always felt it as sweltering hot. Another girl in our experiment . . . invariably impressed her judges as seductive. Even when she wanted to be angry, men whistled at her.[1]

Nonverbal communication is continuous, powerful, and easily misunderstood. Consequently, if we're going to build our families God's way, we must work at carefully sending and receiving nonverbal messages. Families are often devastated by failure in this aspect of their relationships. Don't let it happen to you.

Study and Application Assignments

Do the assignments individually and then discuss your answers with your mate or your study group.

1. Reflect on (or if necessary, review) this chapter and answer the following questions:

   a. What is a general definition of effective communication?

   b. What happens when people don't communicate effectively?

c. Evaluate your family communication in terms of the elements of your definition. Use a rating scale of Excellent, Good, Fair, Poor, Terrible.

d. Why is this chapter titled "I Heard What You Didn't Say"?

e. Give several biblical illustrations of nonverbal communication and note what you can learn from them.

f. Give several extrabiblical examples of nonverbal communication and note what you can learn from them.

g. What does Ephesians 4:28 illustrate about nonverbal communication?

h. Explain the "domino" or "boomerang" concept of nonverbal behavior.

2. Study the following Scripture passages. Note what each one indicates about nonverbal communication. After discussing this with your spouse, summarize what you learned about nonverbal communication.

a. Genesis 3:7-10

b. Genesis 4:5-6

c. Genesis 37:3

d. Genesis 39:4

e. Genesis 40:6, 7

f. Joshua 7:6

g. 1 Samuel 1:4-10

h. 1 Samuel 18:4

i. 1 Kings 19:3, 4a

j. 1 Kings 21:4

k. Proverbs 4:25, 26

l. Proverbs 7:6-9

m. Proverbs 7:10-13a

n. Proverbs 31:12-27

o. Mark 2:3-5

p. Luke 10:30-35a

q. Luke 15:3-4, 8, 20

r. Luke 18:10-13

s. 1 John 3:17

3. Developing marital and family unity requires accurately sending and receiving the right kind of nonverbal messages. First, complete these assignments individually, and then discuss them with each other. Record in writing what comes out of your discussion, and study what you think is important for your own life and family. How do you need to improve in the area of nonverbal communication? Be prepared to share with others.

   a. What are ten nonverbal ways of communicating with another person?

   b. What are some nonverbal behaviors that may hinder the development of a deep and satisfying relationship? Why are they a hindrance?

   c. What nonverbal behaviors may enhance oneness and make marriage and family relations a satisfying experience?

   d. Identify your most problematic nonverbal behaviors and explain how they hinder good family relationships.

   e. What do you consider to be the most common problematic nonverbal behaviors in other family members?

   f. What things do you do nonverbally that encourage a good relationship?

   g. For each family member, identify the nonverbal behaviors that promote good family relationships.

Notes
[1]Ernst Beier, "How We Send Emotional Messages," *Psychology Today*, October 1974, p. 56.

5

How to Hear What's Not Being Said

The story is told about a small town that was predominantly Roman Catholic with a smattering of Jews. Things were not going well there, and so the Roman Catholic leaders decided to ask the Jews to leave. When the leading priest met with the leading rabbi to give him the news, the rabbi challenged the priest to a debate that would decide the fate of the Jews. If the priest won the debate, the Jews would go. But if the rabbi won, the Jews would stay.

The rabbi suggested that they debate only by means of non-verbal communication, and the priest agreed.

When the day of the debate arrived, the priest and rabbi went into a room with a few people who were to decide the winner. The priest stood up and threw his arms open wide. The rabbi responded by vigorously pointing one hand toward the ground. The priest then held up three fingers. The rabbi countered by holding up one finger. Impressed but undeterred, the priest held up an apple. The rabbi took the apple and began to eat it. At this, the priest conceded that he had been outdone. "There's nothing I can do to outwit the rabbi. He has won fair and square. The Jews may stay."

Later the priest explained to his associates what had happened. "I have never met anyone with such finely honed debating skills, such convincing arguments. When I began by throwing my arms open wide, indicating that God is everywhere, he pointed to the ground, meaning that God is also here. I then put up three fingers to declare that God exists in three persons: Father, Son, and Holy Spirit. He responded by holding up one finger to assert that there is only one God. Finally I picked up an apple as a declaration that

God put man to the test. But he took the apple and began to eat it, expressing that man was put to the test and failed. At that point I realized that anything I would say, he could counter with convincing arguments. So I conceded and told him the Jews could stay."

While the priest was recounting what had taken place, the rabbi likewise was asked by his colleagues what had transpired. "I'm not sure," he said. "All I know is that we can stay." When questioned further he explained, "We went into this room and the priest threw open his arms, which meant that we would have to leave. I pointed my hand toward the ground, informing him that we were staying. He then held up three fingers, indicating that we had three days to get out of town. I lifted one finger to declare that we wanted at least a month. Next he offered me an apple conveying his generosity. I grabbed the apple and we had lunch. Don't ask me why, but when I ate the apple, the priest seemed overwhelmed and didn't want to continue. He pronounced me the winner and said that we could stay."

This fictitious story illustrates how easily nonverbal communication can be misunderstood. Not only the priest and the rabbi, but family members can completely misread each other and never realize it. Eliminating or reducing nonverbal miscommunication in the home is an important step in building your family God's way.

To prevent such miscommunication, four important lessons must be learned. We should be concerned about seeing ourselves as others see us.

Know What Others See in You

Each of us needs to learn what and how we are communicating nonverbally to others.

"Facing" the Truth

For example, are you aware of what your facial expression may convey to others? It may be communicating anger when you're not angry at all. You may appear to be so serious and intense that you frighten people. Unless you are aware of what message your face expresses to others, miscommunication can occur, and others may react to an entirely false perception of you.

Several years ago, one of my sons noticed me sitting quietly in the family room and asked, "What's the matter, Dad?" I answered, "Nothing, everything is just fine." "Are you sure nothing is the matter?" he replied. "Yes," I assured him. And after we had a brief conversation, he went on his way.

This occurred a few times (I'm slow to catch on), and I began to wonder why he asked what was the matter. Then I realized that it happened whenever I was deep in thought. As far as I knew, I wasn't upset or angry or anxious at these times. I was just seriously considering an issue in my mind. But all my son saw was the expression on my face, and to him it indicated that I was upset about something.

That experience has helped me to understand how others read me at times. If my facial expressions convey worry or anger or sadness to my son, they probably convey the same thing to others. So I made a decision to be more alert to my facial expressions when I'm around other people. Now when I hear my son coming into the house, I make sure I have a smile on my face and I greet him cheerfully. When I'm counseling, speaking, or just interacting with people, I try to be more aware of what my countenance conveys to others. I don't want to be dishonest or hypocritical by pretending that everything is all right when it isn't. But neither do I want to communicate distress or displeasure when those are not my feelings.

Actions Speak Louder

Recently, Jim (a pseudonym) shared an experience that illustrates the importance of considering the impact our actions have on others. For several years, he lived a double life. He was married, had children, professed to be a Christian, and was active in the church. But at the same time, he was unfaithful to his wife, Tanya, (a pseudonym) and was a practicing homosexual.

In the course of time, the Lord brought him under heavy conviction and gave him a growing concern to become a godly man.

He began to seek help in changing his sinful lifestyle. He first contacted a Christian ministry to homosexuals, which worked with him and then recommended that he seek Christian counseling. He did so and then decided to make a full confession to his pastor and ask him for help. In response, his pastor said: "That's serious and I want to help you. Let's meet together at least once a week."

Jim was thrilled, but do you know how often that pastor met with him? Once! After that, he never set up another appointment and never checked to see how Jim and Tanya were doing. They knew they needed support, encouragement, and accountability. They thought they could count on his help as they worked through the hard problems and made the hard adjustments. But when several weeks had gone by without any action by the pastor, Jim and Tanya began to question if he really cared. His failure to follow through suggested that he did not. And they were left to wonder why. Didn't he know that they were struggling? Was he suffering from homophobia? Was he angry with Jim and unwilling to forgive his duplicity? They felt rejected, unwanted, and alone.

Jim's counselor advised him to talk with his pastor and share his feelings of abandonment. The pastor apologized, saying he hadn't realized how important the proposed meetings were to Jim and his wife. He thought that since they were going to a Christian counselor who knew far more about homosexuality and problematic marriages, he might just get in the way. He himself had little experience working with homosexuals and no success. He stressed that his inaction did not reveal a lack of concern for them.

Probably what the pastor said was true. But he unfortunately had not realized how Jim and Tanya might interpret the discrepancy between his verbal commitment and his failure to follow through (his nonverbal behavior). The pastor knew his reasons for what he was doing and appears to have assumed that they would view it the same way. But they didn't!

Learn from this the need to see how others may read your nonverbal behavior. Insofar as it is possible, make sure that your nonverbal behavior communicates to others what you want to communicate, what you are actually thinking and feeling.

Keep in Touch with Yourself

There are other kinds of communication gaps too. Sometimes what we express externally *does* represent what is going on inside us, but we are out of touch with our own true feelings. This often happens when we experience sinful emotions. Reluctant to acknowledge the possibility that our thoughts, feelings, desires, and values may be wrong (Prov. 16:2; 21:2), we may practice denial, blameshifting, excuse making, covering up, or relabeling. We may deceive ourselves and others (James 1:22) about what is really happening in our lives.

Suppose we are angry. Rather than acknowledge it, we may use diversionary techniques to deflect the truth. Perhaps we flat out deny that we are angry. If someone asks us, "What's bothering you?" we say, "Nothing." When someone says: "You seem very irritated with me. Are you angry about something I've done?" we say: "No, I'm not annoyed. I really love you. How could you get the idea that I don't want you around?" We think that it's safer to deny what we feel than to be honest about our feelings and to deal with them biblically.

Renaming or relabeling our feelings is another way we evade the truth about them. Instead of acknowledging that we are very bitter, resentful, or angry, we use euphemisms such as, "I'm a little hurt," or "I'm disappointed," or "I'm just concerned," or "I don't understand." To protect ourselves from unpleasantness, we minimize the seriousness of what we are experiencing. We may even lose touch with our true feelings, insisting that we're not annoyed, irritated, or angry, when indeed we are. Jeremiah warns us that our hearts are so deceitful that we often don't even know the truth about ourselves (Jer. 17:9). On the surface, denying or relabeling our true feelings may appear to put us at an advantage. In reality, it is a highly dangerous practice.

God's Word exposes the folly and peril of denial and renaming when it says:

> Like an earthen vessel overlaid with silver dross are burning lips and a wicked heart. He who hates disguises it with his lips, but he lays up deceit in his heart. When he speaks graciously, do not believe him, for there are seven abominations in his heart. Though

his hatred covers itself with guile, his wickedness [i.e. his true inner feelings, his hatred, his resentment, his malice] will be revealed [i.e., perhaps by his actions or his facial expressions or gestures] before the assembly [i.e., in public, externally]. A lying tongue [i.e., saying, "I love you, I'm not angry, I'm only hurt," when these words do not reflect one's true experience] hates those it crushes, and a flattering mouth works ruin. (Prov. 26:23-26, 28)

To communicate effectively with other family members, you absolutely must be honest about your thoughts, desires, and emotions. Not that you should necessarily *express* all of them to the rest of the family. But you must express them to yourself, to God, and perhaps to another godly person who may help you deal with them rightly (Gal. 6:1, 2; Heb. 3:12, 13). That means you must learn how to replace unbiblical and ungodly feelings with ones that are biblical and Christ-honoring (Gal. 5:19-26; Eph. 4:17-24; Col. 3:5-14). (How to express your true feelings to others will be discussed in chapters 6 through 9.)

Know When to Explain

Explaining the meaning of your nonverbal behavior to others is an essential part of effective communication. If you're angry about something that happened at work, when you come home, say to your wife: "Honey, this has been some kind of day. Nothing seemed to go right. I'm way behind schedule, and the boss is making unreasonable demands. I'm trying to respond to what has happened in a godly fashion. Right now, though, I'm struggling. I want you and the children to know that if I'm not as cheerful as I should be, it's not because I'm upset with you. I'm also asking you to be a little easy on me tonight. I don't want to be nasty, but I feel like it wouldn't take much to push me over the edge. I'm not excusing myself. But I'm asking for your help until I get this under control."

I know from personal experience how helpful this practice can be. Recently, when I came home from work out of sorts, I tried it with my own family. Before dinner, they expressed their concern and listened to me. During dinner, they prayed for me and were especially gracious and kind. My wife recommended that I take a relaxing bath and listen to some music. I followed her advice, spent some time in prayer, and came away feeling much more relaxed.

Had I not explained my inner struggle, my family may have misread any glum or sinful actions as being directed against them. Their responses may have exacerbated my original distress. In this case, my explanation prevented damaging miscommunication from occurring. It helped my family to bear my burden and be a part of the solution.

Interpret Others' Actions with Care

Thus far our discussion has been aimed at the communication sender. There is, however, an obvious implication for the person on the receiving end of nonverbal communication. If, as we have observed, nonverbal communication is frequently misunderstood by the receiver, it follows that we must be cautious in our interpretation of another person's actions. Love "is not proud" (1 Cor. 13:4, NIV). Love "is not easily angered" (1 Cor. 13:5, NIV). "Love does not delight in evil" (1 Cor. 13:6, NIV). Love "always hopes" (1 Cor. 13:7, NIV). Love puts the best possible interpretation on the other person's behavior. Until proven wrong, love assumes the best rather than the worst. Love doesn't go around looking for insults and offenses. Love is not defensive. Love doesn't take everything personally.

Love recognizes that the same behavior may mean different things in different circumstances. So if we are concerned about what someone's actions are communicating, we might do well to go to that person and say: "You seem distressed. Is there anything that I can help you with? Is there something that is upsetting you?"

Suppose I come home upset and my wife senses that something is bothering me. She doesn't know what it is. All she knows is that I'm not very excited to see her. I kiss her perfunctorily and I'm somewhat withdrawn. I don't respond very well to her attempts to find out about my day or to share hers with me. She gets the idea that I'm annoyed about something.

At that point the evening can go in one of two directions. If I don't explain my behavior, as in the earlier example, my wife might assume that my upset is directed at her. She might compound the problem by taking my actions personally. Or she might reason: "It's evident that something is bothering Wayne. I'd better pray for him and try to cheer him up. Maybe he just needs to be left alone until he unwinds. No, I don't think that's the best thing to do. In the past, Wayne usually has felt better when I've asked him a few questions and helped him get it off his chest."

And so my wife might gently say: "When you came in the house, you looked like a man who had something on his mind. Want to share it with me? Please help me to understand what's going on in you."

With this response my wife would have suspended judgment of my nonverbal behavior until she could ascertain what it meant. By seeking clarification she would have discovered that my actions had nothing to do with her. As a result she could have helped me to respond to whatever was bothering me in a more godly way. If, on the other hand, my actions were a sinful response to something she had done, we could have discussed the issue and resolved it in a God-honoring way. At least we would have avoided the danger of miscommunication because my wife would rightly have understood what was happening.

Clarification—gently asking the other person to help you understand—is a useful technique for increasing the effectiveness of nonverbal communication. Never assume that you understand infallibly what another person's negative nonverbal behavior means. Others have misunderstood you; it's possible that you can misunderstand them. So make the practice of clarification a regular part of your family life.

As good as this practice is for effective communication, let me give you a word of caution. Don't overdo it! Some people are so insecure and sensitive that they constantly think the other person is upset with them. They are hypervigilant to anything that may indicate distress, and they take it personally. They badger the other person with questions: "Do you love me? Have I done something wrong? Are you angry with me? I know something is the matter; you just won't share it with me." As a result, the other person's patience is tried, and he is tempted to become irritated. He feels as if he is being given the third degree. So be moderate in your requests for clarification. Employ the technique carefully when important issues in your relationship are at stake.

Jacob and Esau

Scripture offers an interesting illustration of the importance of clarification. It comes from the life of Jacob at the time of his return to the land where he was born and raised. We must remember that he had left his homeland under bitter circumstances. Because Jacob had cheated and deceived him, his brother Esau had become very angry with him. In fact, he had threatened to kill him. Now Jacob is returning to the region where his brother lived. Unsure of what his brother's attitude will be, he suspects that Esau may still hold a grudge. And so Scripture says:

> Jacob sent messengers ahead of him to his brother Esau in the land of Seir, in the country of Edom. . . . When the messengers returned to Jacob, they said, "We went to your brother Esau, and now he is coming to meet you and four hundred men are with him." (Gen. 32:3, 6, NIV)

Jacob puts this news about Esau through his own interpretational grid. Why would Esau take the time to come to meet him? Why would he bring four hundred men with him? He interprets Esau's nonverbal behavior and concludes that Esau is still carrying a grudge. He hears what Esau isn't saying and decides that Esau wants to wipe him out. The account continues:

> In great fear and distress Jacob divided the people who were with him into two groups, and the flocks and herds and camels as well. He thought, "If Esau comes and attacks one group, the group that is left may escape." Then Jacob prayed, "O God of my father Abraham, God of my father Isaac. . . . Save me, I pray, from the hand of my brother Esau, for I am afraid he will come and attack me. . . ."
> He spent the night there, and from what he had with him he selected a gift for his brother Esau: two hundred female goats and twenty male goats, two hundred ewes and twenty rams, thirty

female camels with their young, forty cows and ten bulls, and twenty female donkeys and ten male donkeys. He put them in the care of his servants ... and said ... "Go ahead of me, and keep some space between the herds." ... He also instructed ... all the others who followed the herds: "You are to say ... to Esau when you meet him ... 'Your servant Jacob is coming behind us.'" For he thought, "I will pacify him with these gifts. ..."

Jacob looked up and there was Esau, coming with his four hundred men.... He himself went on ahead and bowed down to the ground seven times as he approached his brother. (Gen. 32:7-9, 11, 13-16, 19-20; 33:1-3, NIV)

Notice how Jacob's interpretation of Esau's nonverbal behavior influenced him. It influenced his emotions: he became very fearful and distressed. It dominated his thoughts: he spent his time planning how he would respond, what he could do to protect himself, what he and his servants should say. It affected his attitudes and actions: he recognized his own vulnerability; he turned to prayer. He talked constantly about it; he divided his flocks; he became generous and solicitous; he sent a large gift ahead of him to Esau; he bowed down to the ground seven times, evidencing complete submission. All of this took place before Esau had said a word. And, as it turned out, all of this was the result of a misinterpretation. Jacob had misread Esau's nonverbal behavior completely. Scripture tells us:

Esau ran to meet Jacob and embraced him; he threw his arms around his neck and kissed him. And they wept. ... Esau asked, "What do you mean by all these droves I met?" "To find favor in your eyes, my lord," he said. But Esau said, "I already have plenty, my brother. Keep what you have for yourself." (Gen. 33:4, 8-9, NIV)

Clarification and explanation helped Jacob and Esau to avoid misjudging each other's actions. At first, each was unsure of what the other meant. "I am afraid he [Esau] will come and attack me." "What do you [Jacob] mean by all these droves?" They reached a new understanding when they clarified and explained their nonverbal behavior.

But suppose Jacob's first impressions had caused him to retreat to the place he had come from. He would have lived the rest of his days thinking Esau still hated him. He would never have had the blessing of reconciling with his brother. This wrong interpretation would have troubled him to the grave. Or suppose he had decided to get Esau before Esau got him. He might have ambushed his brother before they had a chance to clarify matters. Many lives and possessions might have been lost. He and Esau might both have died without knowing how badly they had misunderstood one another. But all of that was avoided because they took the opportunity for clarification and explanation.

Researchers suggest that communication is 55 percent nonverbal and 45 percent verbal. Whether these percentages are always accurate I don't know. But it is evident that what people hear through our actions is powerful, perhaps more powerful than what we actually say with words.

Seek to develop an honesty about what you are really thinking and feeling. Conscientiously try to see yourself as others might see you. Make the practices of explanation and clarification a regular part of your family life.

Study and Application Assignments

Complete these assignments individually and then discuss your answers with your mate or your study group.

1. Jot down the four important lessons about nonverbal communication that should be learned and practiced in your family. Evaluate yourself as a nonverbal communicator in terms of how well you practice these four principles. Rate yourself on this scale: Excellent; Good; Fair; Poor; Terrible. Do the same for other family members.

2. How can people's responses help us to understand our nonverbal behavior? What may we learn about ourselves if we find that many people are responding to us in a similar way? Consider the implications of Proverbs 11:27; 12:24; 13:15; 13:18; 14:22b; 14:35; 17:13; 22:5; and 27:18 as you formulate your answer.

3. What danger do Proverbs 16:2; 26:23-28; Jeremiah 17:9; and James 1:22;

warn against in the realm of nonverbal behavior?

4. Make a list of feelings or attitudes you have experienced during the past two weeks (e.g., anger, sadness, discouragement, discontentment, joy, happiness, pleasure, peace, worry, despair, contentment, excitement, compassion, frustration, nervousness, fear, terror, annoyance, pride, humiliation, shame, embarrassment, etc.). Note the circumstances connected with each emotional experience. Which of these emotions or attitudes are most problematic to you? Which of them would those who know you well think you experience most frequently? How do these emotions or attitudes affect your nonverbal behavior? How would others know (guess) that you were experiencing one of these emotions or attitudes if you didn't tell them?

5. How do the truths taught by certain phrases in 1 Corinthians 13:4-7 relate to the issue of interpreting someone else's nonverbal behavior?

6. How does the example of Jacob and Esau illustrate the main point about nonverbal communication presented in this chapter?

7. Pick six emotions or attitudes listed below, and try to communicate them by nonverbal means alone. Picture yourself in a situation where you have experienced the emotion or attitude you are trying to depict. Take turns with your partner until each of you has enacted six emotions or attitudes. See how often you can guess what the other person is trying to communicate. Discuss the results.

Love	Sadness	Hurt
Anger	Unbelief	Trust
Happiness	Doubt	Confidence
Sexual Interest	Indifference	Pride
Peace	Apathy	Embarrassment
Frustration	Humility	Anguish
Uneasiness	Anxiety	Excitement
Irritation	Guilt	Delight
Fear	Cautiousness	Pleasure
Discouragement	Shame	

6

Small Talk: The Silent Menace

"Whenever my wife and I get into a discussion that would help me get to know her better, she just clams up and refuses to talk. She keeps everything bottled up."

"My wife seldom initiates a conversation. If I didn't take the lead in almost every conversation, it would be like a morgue around our house."

"My husband has one word in his vocabulary. No, he actually has two. One is Uh-huh and the other is Uh-uh."

"You've heard of old stoneface. Well, I married it."

"I married a newspaper with legs on it."

"Getting our son to talk is like pulling teeth. If I ask him a question, he just grunts or gives a one-word answer. His favorite words are 'nothing' or 'I don't know' or 'get out of my face.' Other children talk to their parents. Why can't he?"

Every marriage and family counselor has heard people speak painfully about communication breakdowns like these. Multitudes of people, both men and women, long for more sharing from other family members, but a dominant pattern of what I call "small talk" keeps them at a distance. I'm not referring to small talk in the sense of light, introductory conversation, but talk that is small in quantity.

The Worth of Words

God has designed us to communicate verbally, and he expects us to do so. The following are a few of many verses encouraging us to use the gift of speech and in effect warning us of "small talk."

79

> The mouth of the righteous is a fountain of life. . . . (Prov. 10:11)
>
> The lips of the righteous nourish many. . . . (Prov. 10:21, NIV)
>
> The mouth of the righteous brings forth wisdom. . . . (Prov. 10:31, NIV)
>
> The tongue of the wise brings healing. . . . (Prov. 12:18)
>
> Speak to one another. . . . (Eph. 5:19, NIV)
>
> Encourage each other with these words. (1 Thess. 4:18, NIV)

All of these verses indicate that God wants us to utilize our ability to speak. The lips of the righteous man aren't supposed to be continuously silent; they're to be put to work nourishing others. Our mouths are to be used to bring cheer, to turn away wrath, to establish friendships, to commend knowledge, to sustain the weary, to give encouragement, and to promote healing.

When God describes the model wife and mother, he says, "She opens her mouth with wisdom, and the teaching of kindness is on her tongue" (Prov. 31:26). She doesn't keep her mouth shut all the time. Her husband and children know what she is thinking and feeling because she tells them. They don't have to guess or depend exclusively on her nonverbal behavior. This woman shares, and her openness promotes harmony and closeness with other members of the family.

Every home needs a healthy amount of verbal communication among family members. Prayerful planning and Spirit-empowered action can make this a reality.

Forms of Small Talk

Word Deficit

Perhaps the most common manifestation of "small talk" or what I sometimes call "undertalk" is simply a lack of words. I've had people tell me that their families have gone for days without uttering a word. One man indicated that his wife had not said a word to him in five weeks. Parents have told me of children who will not initiate a conversation. They speak only if they are asked a question and even then very sparingly. When such patterns exist, the relationship stays on a very superficial level and becomes boring. There is something exciting about sharing verbally.

In my workday I sometimes teach counseling several hours at a time. I occasionally grow tired and feel like relaxing or calling it a day, but can't because I still have counseling cases scheduled.

On such occasions, I've wondered if I could be of any value to my counselees. But the appointments have been made, and the people have come. So I ask the Lord for help and give my attention to the people. I listen to what they say and respond to them. They respond to me in turn, and about fifteen minutes into the session I realize that I am not tired anymore. My counselees' willingness to open their lives, their inner selves to me is rejuvenating. Often I finish the sessions with more energy than when I began.

I've often had the same experience with my family. Discontentment, fatigue, and loneliness have been relieved through interpersonal sharing. A sense of excitement, involvement, security, warmth, and affirmation has grown out of my interaction with them.

But "undertalk" has the reverse effect. When one woman told me that her husband was very uncommunicative, I suggested: "Well, maybe this communication deficiency has nothing to do with you. Perhaps he finds it very difficult to talk to anyone." My point was not to excuse the husband or to minimize the wife's concerns. But I know from experience that some people simply find it more difficult to communicate than others.

She disagreed, however. "No, I've watched him when he is around other people, especially the people with whom he works. With them he has plenty to say. It's just with me that he closes up." This woman interpreted her husband's "small talk" as a rejection of her. "He must not think I'm very important. I'm not even worth talking to." Her husband's unwillingness even to make an effort to communicate provoked a spirit of frustration, discontentment, and dissatisfaction within her.

Topic Avoidance

In some instances "undertalk" is manifested by topic avoidance. A person may talk about certain things but not others. Perhaps he will talk about what interests him, but not what interests others.

Or he will gladly discuss superficial things, but won't share his thoughts, opinions, or feelings.

That is a tragedy. Scripture informs us that "pleasant words are ... sweet to the soul" and that sharing good news is "like cold water to a weary soul" (Prov. 16:24; 25:25). Some of the best news and most refreshing words that family members could share with each other are pleasant words such as "I love you," "You're really special to me," "I thank God for you," or "I really enjoy being with you."

Regrettably, many people are reluctant to verbalize such sentiments to members of their family. I often hear counselees say something like: "I love her in my heart. Down deep inside, I really do. I just don't go around saying it." One woman told me that her husband had not told her he loved her in four years. I asked him if that was true. He answered, yes. "Why? Don't you love her?" I inquired. He replied: "Oh sure, I love her. I just don't talk about it. I show it in other ways."

Many a child (young or old) has expressed with great pain and sadness, "My parents have never told me they love me." Hurting parents make similar statements about their children. I have seen them weep in anguish over children who neither verbalized nor demonstrated love to them.

Jim was frustrated because his wife Jane would not communicate with him on several important family issues. Topics such as sex, child discipline, in-law relationships, finances, job changes, or similar problems were off limits. When Jim would try to stimulate a discussion on some of these issues, Jane would simply say, "I don't want to talk about it," or "Let's talk about it tomorrow," or "I really haven't given it any thought." At times she would become annoyed or give a flippant answer making it clear that she didn't want to discuss it further. The more Jane excelled at topic avoidance, the more unresolved issues accumulated over the years. Eventually Jim and Jane experienced serious marital and family dysfunction because of this failure to address many important issues.

Apathetic Talk

"Small talk" sometimes is disguised in the form of apathetic talk. The message "I don't care what you think or feel or want or say" can be communicated literally, or it can be conveyed indirectly by a blank expression, inattention, or a lack of enthusiasm in your voice when a family member shares his interests or concerns. In one way or another, the message comes across that you really don't care what the other person is saying; you are indifferent to him and his ideas.

Deficient Sharing

Deficient personal sharing is another way that "small talk" displays itself. Wives frequently say something like this: "I don't know my husband. He doesn't share his thoughts. He doesn't express his desires or his goals or his concerns. He doesn't display his feelings. He keeps me at a distance and doesn't allow me to get to know what's going on inside of him. I want to know what makes him tick, but he won't let me."

Sometimes parents will say: "I really don't know what my child is thinking or how he feels about things. He's like a house with most of the doors locked and most of the curtains pulled so I can't see in." Deficient sharing prevents intimacy and hinders efforts to build your family God's way.

Acknowledgment Deficit

"Small talk" sometimes promotes family destruction by means of acknowledgment deficit. Steve has what he thinks is a great idea. It is very important to him, so he shares it with his father, expecting: "Hey, Steve, that's a terrific idea! How can I be of help to you?" or at least: "That's very interesting. Tell me more." Instead there is no response, or merely a "hmm." Then Dad picks up the newspaper or changes the conversation to a topic important to himself. It's as if Steve hasn't said anything—at least anything worthy of attention. As a result, Steve feels rejected.

Acknowledgment deficit may occur during family discussions, when one member makes a contribution, but no one else pays any attention. Or perhaps the suggestion is rejected in a cavalier fashion. It happens when one member of the family parades the ideas or accomplishments of another as if they were his own, refusing to acknowledge the true source. It may take place when family members have argued or one person has sinned against another and no one acknowledges fault or error. When the words, "I was wrong and you were right" or "Please forgive me for the sinful way I treated you" are seldom heard among family members, you have acknowledgment deficit in the home.

Appreciation Deficit

"Small talk" also manifests itself in families suffering from chronic deficit in expressions of appreciation. In such homes family members routinely take each other for granted, seldom if ever thanking one another for simple kindnesses. They act as if they deserve the help and consideration they receive from each other. Favors are considered to be the other person's duty.

Maybe some family member has done his utmost to please another. He or she has been extremely faithful in fulfilling responsibilities and cheerful in going the extra mile. Yet no one gives recognition or shows gratitude. Some wives, husbands, parents, and children never hear other family members say "Thank you" to them. They are treated like servants who shouldn't expect recognition for service. Whatever they do is merely their job—their responsibility. And why should they be thanked for doing that?

Significantly, most of the letters of the apostle Paul contained some expression of thanks or appreciation, not only to God, but also for and to the people to whom he wrote. To the Philippians he wrote, "I thank my God every time I remember you. . . . because of your partnership in the gospel from the first day until now"; "I rejoice greatly in the Lord that . . . you have renewed your concern for me"; you are "my joy and my crown" (Phil. 1:3, 5; 4:10, 1, NIV). Paul didn't take for granted these brethren or what they had done for him. True, they had only done what they should have done as Christians. Yet he made it a point to express his gratitude to them.

No Christian family that takes God and his Word seriously should allow "undertalk" in the form of a lack of commendation to rule the day. We are to encourage one another, esteem one another, and appreciate one another (1 Thess. 5:14; Phil. 2:3; Rom. 12:10). This is our Christian duty. It is also a means of promoting good family relationships. People who appreciate and respect one another enjoy each other and tend to experience harmony and unity with each other.

Reasons for Small Talk

We've seen the manifestations of "small talk." A more perplexing question for many is How does "small talk" establish itself in the home? I've observed six common contributors to "small talk."

Fatigue

Sometimes cranking up a conversation is real work. You attempt to communicate, but it seems there is a barrier between you and the other person. You make one attempt and nothing clicks. And so you have to try again and again, which takes effort. Some people aren't willing to expend that much energy, and so "small talk" gets a foothold in the family.

Selfish Vindictiveness

Selfishness, stubbornness, and a desire to punish are the roots of "small talk's" power in other families.

"I don't care if other family members want me to communicate more. All I want is what I want!"

"Nobody is going to tell me what to do. She'll have to accept me the way I am. She wants me to communicate, but I'm not going to give in to her because if I do, she'll take advantage of me."

"I'll show them. They want me to talk. Well, I'm not going to! They don't do a lot of things I want them to do. They hurt me! They don't let me do what I want to do! I've got no other way to get even, but if I keep quiet, that really bugs them."

A Sense of Inferiority

In some instances "small talk" takes up residence in the home because someone has a sense of inferiority. A person feels he has nothing worth saying. He develops the idea that everybody else is much smarter than he is. He's afraid that if he opens his mouth, he might sound foolish. So a sense of inferiority (or is it pride?) keeps him from talking.

Fear

Similarly, fear invites "small talk" into family relationships. People hesitate to speak freely because they fear that others may use what they say against them. They realize that if they keep their talk on a superficial level, there isn't much risk, but if they really open up and share their innermost secrets, others might laugh at them. Or if they share some of their struggles and temptations, someone may look down his nose at them and say: "You're supposed to be spiritual and you're struggling with that temptation? Good Christians don't do that."

"Fear of man will prove to be a snare, but whoever trusts in the Lord is kept safe" (Prov. 29:25, NIV). Family members may be so afraid of the ridicule, disagreement, or rejection of their relatives that they refuse to share their thoughts or discuss certain issues. That was Jane's problem, mentioned earlier. Viewing disagreement as rejection, she despised controversy of any kind. She needed help in realizing that this was wrong. More than that, she needed help in developing her relationship with God: "Whoever trusts in the Lord is kept safe"; "In the fear of the Lord there is strong confidence" (Prov. 14:26). That realization was the key to Jane's overcoming the problem of "small talk." Putting her trust in God, recognizing that God was her sufficiency and security, developing a truly God-focused life enabled her to put aside her paralyzing fear of man.

According to Proverbs, an inordinate fear of man indicates distrust in God and an attempt to find our security in something other than him. A vital and appropriate fear of God invariably delivers us from ungodly inhibitions and paralyzing fears. It frees us to do what is right, regardless of the apparent consequences. It allows us to talk with family members about things that are important for the family to function properly and experience harmony and unity.

Rejection by others may be extremely painful. However, if we are secure in our relationship with God, there's a sense in which it really doesn't matter what others think of us or how they respond.

"If God is for us, who [or what] is against us?" (Rom. 8:31). "The Lord is my light and my salvation; whom shall I fear? The Lord is the defense of my life; whom shall I dread?" (Ps. 27:1).

Past Training

Some people have learned "small talk" from their past training. The old idea that "children are meant to be seen, not heard," still holds court in some families. Instead of teaching them when and how to speak and when to be silent, parents teach their children (by verbal and nonverbal instruction) that good little boys or girls keep quiet and don't interfere. Children learn that being silent pleases Mom and Dad. The less a child says, the better.

A number of years ago, a friend from another part of the world came to visit us. One evening our whole family was sitting around the dinner table with him when he broached some theological issues. He looked at me and I shared my viewpoint. Then my son Chip respectfully injected his comments. At an appropriate time and in an appropriate manner, Nathan added his perspective. I suspect (though I don't remember) that my daughter Beth may have also contributed a few remarks. Josh was still a baby, and my wife Carol was out in the kitchen, or they probably would have entered into the conversation too.

I considered their input entirely proper and worthwhile. They didn't interrupt. They were not rude or smart-alecky. Nor were they loud, and they did not dominate the conversation. They made a good contribution to what I thought was a discussion, not a monologue.

But my friend saw it another way. He was disturbed that children would enter an adult conversation. He made that clear to us and even mentioned it to someone else. In his mind, "Children are meant to be seen, not heard," or perhaps neither seen nor heard.

We've always encouraged family discussion of most issues and welcomed the insights and opinions of our children. God has taught us much through them. Certainly children need to be trained—but not to avoid talking. Instead of "small talk," far better to train them in "right talk." Teach your children to talk about the right things, in the right way, and at the right time. Train them to speak respectfully, thoughtfully, constructively, and under control. This is all part of building our families God's way.

My point is not that adults enmeshed in "small talk" because of past training lack the natural ability to communicate effectively. They just were trained not to use that ability. Now they need to train themselves by following the guidelines in this book for becoming better communicators.

Busyness

Busyness is one of the most common contributors to "small talk" in the home. People say: "I'd talk more if only I had the time. Someday, when I'm older and don't have to work as hard or as long, I'll talk to my mate or my children, but I can't find the time right now. I'm too busy making a living, going to church, taking care of things around the house. When am I supposed to find the time to talk to my spouse and the children?"

Makes sense, doesn't it? Not at all. God's Word declares communication to be extremely important, and we neglect it at great peril. Besides that, human experience abundantly illustrates the destructiveness of "small talk" in families and marriages. Building deep, God-honoring, satisfying family relationships requires an adequate amount of effective communication.

The person who continuously uses his busyness as an excuse for "small talk" either doesn't want communication or is ignorant of its importance in his life and family. He either doesn't know or doesn't care about what God says on the subject. In reality, the person shows that there are a lot of other things that are more important (and perhaps enjoyable) to him than communicating with his mate and children. We make time for what we value most in life. Other things are left undone.

If you believe the Bible, you simply can't read what it says about communication and come away with the idea that effective and adequate communication is optional in family life. Nor can you observe what happens in families after many years of "small talk" and regard it as harmless. "Small talk" is a family killer. God's Word declares it, and human experience illustrates it.

Overcoming "Small Talk"

If "small talk" is a destroyer, how can you overcome "small talk" and increase your verbal communication with family members?

1. You must *want* to overcome "small talk." Growth in any area of life usually doesn't occur by accident. It happens because people are willing to work at it. Many people who were poor conversationalists have experienced great change because they were willing to work at improving. To the paralyzed man in John 5 Jesus said, "Do you want to be made well? Well then, take up your bed and walk." To those inhibited in the area of communication, Jesus would say: "Do you want to become a better communicator? If you do, I'll help, but you must want to improve and must be willing to make an effort."

2. You must make overcoming "small talk" a regular matter of prayer. "Be anxious for nothing, but in [and for] everything by prayer and supplication with thanksgiving let your requests be made known to God" (Phil. 4:6). With God's help you can change. You may never become the best communicator in the world, but God can help you to become the conversationalist he wants you to be. If you will trust and obey him, you can count on God's help to improve, and you may pray with confidence that he will hear and answer.

Prayer is beneficial in developing communication skills in at least two ways. First, God strengthens and enables us to do his will through prayer. He "is able to do exceeding abundantly beyond all that we ask or think, according to the power that works within us" (Eph. 3:20). "You do not have because you do not ask" is the reminder in James 4:2. "Ask, and it shall be given to you" is the exhortation and promise of our Lord Jesus Christ (Matt. 7:7).

Second, prayer is useful in developing communication skills because as we learn to talk to God and share ourselves with him, we are learning how to communicate with another person. Certainly, the main concern in prayer should not be to practice conversational skills, but that is a side benefit. If you can learn to be open and honest with the God of the universe, you can learn to talk with anyone!

3. Prime your conversational pump. Read magazines, newspapers, the Bible, good books, or other literature. Listen to the radio or watch informative television programs, and discuss what you have learned. You don't have to be original with all you say. Think back

over your life and try to recall interesting things that happened to you during every five- or ten-year period of your life. Occasionally share some of your more interesting experiences with your family. Practice ahead of time; make a daily effort to share something interesting with your family.

4. Make a list of questions to ask people. Include general questions you could ask anyone and specific questions for particular individuals. If need be, put these questions on a 3 x 5 card and carry it with you so that you can sneak a peek when you don't know where to go with a conversation. You may use the time when you're travelling home from work to think and pray about things you will share and questions you will ask family members about their day.

Learning how to ask questions is probably the main secret of becoming a better conversationalist. In her book, *How to Talk with Practically Anybody About Practically Anything*,[1] Barbara Walters, regarded as one of the world's best interviewers, asserts that the key to conversation is to learn how to ask good questions. Watch any good interviewer and you will find that they don't do most of the talking. They have learned what kind of questions to ask, and how, when, and where to ask them.

5. Observe others who are good at communicating effectively and learn from their example. God's method of training us involves showing as well as telling.

6. Make a regular, conscientious effort to put the suggestions for improvement into practice. Your skills as a communicator can be increased, but only if you are willing to practice. Our faculties are trained by reason of practice (Heb. 5:14).

The Tongue-tied Pastor

I was raised on a farm. We got up early in the morning, and worked all day. Much of the time I was alone on the tractor and often worked till late at night. When we ate breakfast, lunch, or dinner, we didn't do much communicating. We wanted to finish eating so we could get out and do the work. As a result, I didn't get much practice communicating. Frankly, I was very poor at it. "Small talk" was the pattern of my life.

When I became a pastor, one of my biggest fears was what I would do on visitation. I wondered, "What will I talk about when I'm sitting all alone with people in their homes? How do I start and keep a conversation going?" Give me a topic I know something about, and I can talk easily with people for hours. But knowing where and how to begin—that was a different matter.

Ironically, the ministry of counseling, to which I now happily devote a large portion of every week, was the second thing I most feared and disliked at the beginning of my ministry. During my first pastorate I avoided counseling as much as possible. I did very little of it for two reasons: I didn't know how to talk with people. And few people wanted to come. They must have sensed my discomfort and ineptness in interpersonal relationships.

I'm still not the world's greatest conversationalist, but with God's help I've made progress in my struggle with "small talk." Communicating is much easier for me now, and I am better able to build my family God's way, as well as minister to others for Jesus Christ. I know I'm more comfortable with people, and they are more comfortable with me. Now, in most instances, I can get a conversation started and keep it going. Rather than fear counseling, I find it something that I really enjoy.

Family Applications

Our family has worked on our communication in many ways too. Since the beginning of our marriage, my wife and I have made it a practice to have at least one date night a week when we could be alone and focus on our relationship. Sometimes we go out; other times we spend the time together at home. We also have a daily communication time. When the children were very young, we did this after they were in bed. (This was one reason why we didn't allow them to stay up as long as we did!)

As the children grew older and stayed up later, we retreated to our bedroom or someplace else where the children could not hear us, and discussed anything that either of us thought should be shared. We gave the children focused attention at other times and informed them that Mom and Dad needed this time to spend with each other. They were told that unless it was an emergency, they were not to interrupt us. And they didn't!

Our daily communication is so important to us that we still guard it carefully. When I must be away from home for a few days, I make it a point to call every day or every other day to touch base with my wife and family. I agree with one preacher who was chided as being wasteful for engaging in this practice. His response: "Telephone calls are sure a lot cheaper and less painful than a divorce."

From the early years, one night a week was set aside as a family night where we could build family relationships and practice communication. Every night at the dinner table, each person was asked to share at least one good or interesting experience that occurred during the day. We also had (and still do, even though there are fewer children living at home these days) regular family devotions during which we read and discussed Scripture and other Christian literature, sang, prayed, and memorized Scripture. Every person was expected to participate in the discussions. Questions, comments, prayer requests, and problems were invited.

From time to time, the leadership of our family discussion time was shared among the family members. Family conference tables were called when special problems arose or when family decisions needed to be made. Anyone could ask for these conference times. Anything that was profitable was fair game for consideration. And all were allowed to—and did—make their contributions. The result? Over the years, practicing family communication has helped me to overcome and my family to avoid the problem of "small talk."

To the Listener

Some of you with a mate, a parent, or a child given to "undertalk" may be asking, "What can I do to help this family member to overcome 'small talk' in his life?"

1. You can pray for the person. Don't put undue pressure on him by frequently reminding him that you are doing so unless he has acknowledged his problem and asked you to pray for him. For the most part, do your praying in private. Ask God to help this

person in whatever way he needs assistance. If fear (acknowledged or unacknowledged) is part of the problem, ask God to free him from that fear, and to enable you and other family members to relate to him in such a way that his fears would be reduced.

2. Provide an atmosphere in which it is safe for him to talk openly, an atmosphere of acceptance and respect where he can share his honest opinions, desires, and feelings without being ridiculed, interrupted, pressured, or responded to with excessive emotions. Don't misunderstand: acceptance and respect aren't necessarily synonymous with approval of all that is said. You don't have to agree with someone to communicate "I respect you; I value you." You can disagree with someone without wiping him out as a person. If you want people to communicate openly and freely, you must make it safe for them to open up to you.

To return to an earlier illustration, Jane refused to discuss important issues with Jim because she didn't like the way he pressured her to conform to his views. She thought that in any discussion she always came off the loser. Sometimes Jim would line up his reasons and present them as if he were a lawyer going to court. Any idea she contributed was summarily shot down. Boisterously he would prove himself right and her wrong.

Jim would strongly deny that this was the case. He could point to time after time when things were done her way. But even when she won, Jane thought she lost, because Jim would act like a martyr or remind her (subtly or not so subtly) of how magnanimous he was. In her mind, Jim didn't want a discussion—he wanted conformity and would coerce or manipulate to get it.

Jim's method of discussion had intensified Jane's fear of rejection, leading her to think it wasn't safe to talk about many issues. In some respects, Jim was reaping what he had sown. And if he wanted to help Jane overcome her fear of discussing certain issues, he needed to create a safer atmosphere for communication to occur. He needed to heed the scriptural admonitions: "Let all bitterness and wrath and anger and clamor and slander be put away from you, along with all malice. And be kind to one another, tender-hearted, forgiving each other, just as God in Christ also has forgiven you" (Eph. 4:31, 32).

Often when a timid person finally gathers all his courage and risks opening up to another family member, he perceives he is rejected or demeaned. Hurt and demoralized, he pulls back into himself. His fear that it's not safe to share his thoughts and feelings is reinforced. "Well, I'm not going to open up like that again," he reasons. "The last time I did I was shot down. I don't need that kind of thing." Eventually this becomes a lifestyle, a habitual way of handling risky issues or situations.

If you have a family member like this, you must learn to listen calmly and respectfully to what he has to say. When your wife opens up about something in your marriage or your life, don't immediately try to correct her or defend yourself. When your husband begins to discuss a problem in his life or your life or your marriage, don't expect the worst or react as if he is intent on making your life miserable. If you do, you'll be encouraging your mate to think it's unsafe to bring up important issues with you.

Listen respectfully and unselfishly. Express appreciation for the other person's willingness to share, and seriously consider what he or she says. Be willing to exercise self-control and keep an open mind. Affirm wherever you can and answer appropriately (more about that in chapters 7-10).

Let me give you an example of what it means to make it safe to talk. On one occasion, we were having a family discussion when Joshua, our youngest, said something that was somewhat funny. Everybody broke out laughing. I looked over at Josh and noticed that he was hanging his head, hurt by our laughter. So I said: "Josh, we aren't laughing at you. We're laughing with you." Josh looked back at me and said, "You're not laughing with me because I'm not laughing." I immediately asked him for forgiveness and assured him that we were sorry for hurting him.

If our family had repeatedly laughed at what Josh said and ignored his feelings, we would have discouraged him from taking part in family discussions. Family members need to know that it's safe to share what's on their hearts. They need to know that home is a place of refuge and safety, a place where people love you, care for you, and respect you (Prov. 14:26). In Christ, that is possible for every home.

As indicated by the title of this chapter, "small talk" is a menace to constructive, God-honoring family relationships. It can be a serious impediment to building a family God's way. With God's help, it must and can be eliminated as people identify the forms of and reasons for its existence in their families and implement the guidelines for overcoming it delineated in this chapter.

Study and Application Assignments

Do the assignments individually, then discuss your answers with your mate or your study group.

1. Note what the following verses say about the positive value of words. Consider what using speech in the way described could mean in building your family God's way. Notice why "small talk" or "undertalk" is a hindrance to healthy family relationships. Follow the example given for Proverbs 10:21 below:

   a. Proverbs 10:21: Words can nourish or build up other people; since people appreciate the person who nourishes them, words are an important means of promoting good family relationships. Since words can nourish, strengthen, and encourage, "small talk" is a serious problem. "Undertalkers" are not contributing to the family as they could and should.

   b. Proverbs 12:18

   c. Proverbs 12:25

   d. Proverbs 15:4

   e. Proverbs 15:7

   f. Proverbs 15:30

   g. Proverbs 31:26

   h. Ecclesiastes 12:11

   i. Isaiah 50:4

   j. Job 4:4

   k. Malachi 3:16

   l. 1 Thessalonians 4:18

2. Reflect on the teaching of this chapter and answer these questions:

   a. What forms of "small talk" are mentioned in this chapter?

   b. Are there other forms of "undertalk" that you have observed? Describe them.

   c. Evaluate the impact of "small talk" on the people associated with those who practiced it.

   d. What reasons for "undertalk" are mentioned in this chapter?

   e. Can you think of any other reasons for "undertalk"? What are they?

   f. Think through the suggestions for overcoming "small talk." What do you think of these suggestions? Are they appropriate? Can you think of any other suggestions that may also help an "undertalker"?

3. Use the following inventory to evaluate yourself on different kinds of "undertalk" or "small talk": 4 = never; 3 = seldom; 2 = sometimes; 1 = often; 0 = usually. Circle the number that is true of you.

a. General lack of words	4 3 2 1 0
b. Topic avoidance	4 3 2 1 0
c. Apathetic talk	4 3 2 1 0
d. Deficient personal sharing	4 3 2 1 0
e. Acknowledgment deficit	4 3 2 1 0
f. Appreciation deficit	4 3 2 1 0
g. Other_____	4 3 2 1 0

   Total the number of 2s: ___ (need for some improvement).
   Total the number of 1s: ___ (need for more improvement).
   Total the number of 0s: ___ (need for major improvement).

4. Use the following inventory to evaluate any areas in which your family may practice "small talk": 1 = quantity is just right; 0 = quantity is too little.

a. Spiritual issues, church, devotions, Bible truths, prayer, Christian service, etc.	1 0
b. Facts, information	1 0
c. Ideas, opinions	1 0
d. Feelings	1 0
e. Desires, concerns, interests	1 0
f. Plans, goals	1 0
g. Dreams, aspirations	1 0
h. Finances, material things, purchases, savings, investments	1 0

i. Work, school   1   0
j. Sexual matters, desires, likes, dislikes   1   0
k. Friends   1   0
l. Recreation, sports, vacations, relaxation   1   0
m. Problems, failures   1   0
n. Joys, victories, successes   1   0
o. What you read, study, learn, hear, see   1   0
p. Current events, politics   1   0
q. Other_____   1   0

Note items on which you think there is too little talk. Discuss with your mate and family whether or not they agree and what can be done to improve in these areas.

5. Reflect on whether you or some family member practices "small talk," and seek to identify the reason(s) behind your "undertalk."

Yes/ No/ Maybe

a. Topic deficit   ___ ___ ___
b. Inferiority   ___ ___ ___
c. Tiredness   ___ ___ ___
d. Fear   ___ ___ ___
e. Past training   ___ ___ ___
f. Past experiences   ___ ___ ___
g. Busyness   ___ ___ ___
h. Ignorance about the importance   ___ ___ ___
i. Punishment   ___ ___ ___
j. Selfishness   ___ ___ ___
k. Stubbornness   ___ ___ ___
l. Other _____   ___ ___ ___

6. If you have identified the forms of "small talk" to which you are prone and the reasons behind this pattern, discuss with your mate and family how you will implement the suggestions for overcoming them. Add anything you think would be helpful, and then follow through on them.

Notes
[1]Barbara Walters, *How to Talk with Practically Anybody About Practically Anything* (New York: Dell, 1978).

7

Enough Is Enough
and Too Much Is Too Much

Contrary to the old saying, you *can* get too much of a good thing. Sleep, rest, and relaxation are good things, but of the person who overindulges in any of them, Scripture asks: "How long will you lie down, O sluggard? When will you arise from your sleep?" Such a person responds: "A little sleep, a little slumber, a little folding of the hands to rest. . . ." But Scripture warns him, "Your poverty will come in like a vagabond, and your need like an armed man" (Prov. 6:9-11). Food too is a good thing, but eating too much food can cause major problems. According to Scripture, "The glutton will come to poverty" (Prov. 23:21).

Many good things become destructive when they are overdone, even communication in the home. The Bible often indicates that "overtalk" can be a destructive practice. "When there are many words, transgression is unavoidable" (Prov. 10:19). Proverbs 11:12 emphasizes the same point: "He who despises his neighbor lacks sense, but a man of understanding keeps silent." Proverbs 12:23 discourages overtalk by informing us that "a prudent man conceals knowledge, but the heart of fools proclaims folly." Clearly, the fool has an open-mouth policy and is constantly talking.

Proverbs 17 offers several insights into the destructive nature of "overtalk." According to verses 27 and 28: "He who restrains his words has knowledge. . . . Even a fool, when he keeps silent, is considered wise. When he closes his lips, he is counted prudent." Earlier in Proverbs 17 "overtalk" is charged with destroying good relationships: "He who repeats a matter separates intimate friends" (v. 9).

"Overtalk" can destroy friendships, hinder marriages, and cause parent-child relationships to deteriorate. As the writer of Ecclesiastes said, there is a time to speak and there is a time to keep silent (Eccl. 3:7). People who want to build their families God's way must know what, when, and *how much* to speak.

Forms of Overtalk

Monopolizing

Some of the previously cited verses imply that certain people have a propensity to dominate conversations. Any verbal interaction with them becomes a monologue. When someone asks a question, they are the first and often the only persons to give an answer. They find listening to others extremely difficult.

Often an "undertalker" and an "overtalker" will initially attract each other and become married. At first this seems like a good arrangement. The "undertalker" need not try to converse, and the "overtalker" can do all the talking he wants. But then the glitter wears off, and the quiet person either tunes the other person out or becomes resentful that the conversation is so one sided. The overwhelmed and dominated spouse may find it difficult to respect the dominator, and a sense of alienation may result.

Gossip

Proverbs 26:22 describes a second form of "overtalk": "The words of a whisperer are like dainty morsels." The whisperer in this verse is someone who doesn't want certain people to hear what he is saying because he's spreading rumors or slandering someone. He's afraid to speak out loud or to the person about whom he is whispering.

Sometimes family members gossip about other family members. Husband or wives may speak evil of their mates to their children, their parents, their siblings, or their friends in an attempt to win sympathy or approval. Perhaps upset by something their mates are or aren't doing, they tell other people how terribly they are being treated. Often under the guise of wanting prayer or counsel, in reality they want sympathy, agreement, or approval.

I'm not speaking here about the legitimate sharing of family problems when (1) biblical attempts have been made to resolve the difficulties and have failed, (2) the person's motive for sharing is a sincere desire to get help, (3) the person shares only with those who can furnish the godly counseling that will provide solutions (Ps. 1:1, 2), and (4) the information shared may be helpful to others in a preventative, protective, or restorative way. This kind of sharing isn't gossip and is commended by the Word of God (Matt. 18:15, 16; Prov. 15:22; Prov. 18:17; Prov. 11:14; Prov. 12:15; Gal. 6:1-3).

Unfortunately, many individuals share information about other family members in a way that does not meet these criteria. And eventually what goes around tends to come around. The person's mate or child or parent learns that evil reports are being spread about him. He feels betrayed; his confidence in the offending family member is strained. He now wonders if he can trust him or her. Slowly but surely, if this type of gossip isn't dealt with biblically, the relationship deteriorates.

When I was much younger, a wise individual warned me about a person who was sharing some juicy tidbits with me: "Wayne, remember that the dog that will bring a bone will carry a bone as well." People who carry gossip to you will often carry gossip *about* you as well. At first, you may think you are privileged in having this person share private information with you. Later you discover that you have been "had," because you find out that this same person has been spreading evil reports about you to other people.

Even if that doesn't happen, you will find that what began as a "dainty morsel" (Prov. 26:22) ends up being distasteful and repulsive. Because of indwelling sin, we often enjoy a bit of gossip. It seems so pleasant to hear those nasty things about other people that make us look good or at least bring others down to our level. However, what seemed so delicious is really very dangerous, because gossip "go[es] down into the innermost parts of the body" (Prov. 26:22). It gets deep within us and affects us from the inside out. Evil reports we once heard may still affect our attitudes toward people years later.

Scripture says, "Good news puts fat on the bones" (Prov. 15:30) and makes the heart glad (Prov. 12:25). Continuous bad news has the opposite effect. It saddens the heart and gnaws at individuals and relationships. Gossip can tear apart the home.

Defensive Speech

Proverbs 26 gives us a humorous yet realistic word picture of another kind of "overtalk" (Prov. 26:13-16; see also 22:13). We are told about a man who isn't working. He's not going anywhere or doing anything. He is even neglecting some of the necessary functions of life! Scripture says of this man, "As the door turns on its hinges, so does [this man] on his bed." He "buries his hand in the dish; he is weary of bringing it to his mouth again" (Prov. 26:14, 15).

What possible reason can this man give for being so irresponsible, so listless? How will he answer those who ask him, "Why aren't you out there working?" Will he acknowledge that he just doesn't want to work? Will he admit that he is lazy? This man "is wiser in his own eyes than seven men who can give a discreet answer" (Prov. 26:16). He can and does justify whatever he does. As far as he is concerned, all his ways "are clean in his own sight" (Prov. 16:2.). He feels totally justified in what he is doing.

Though seven men may charge him with an indiscretion, and five times God may (and does) call him a sluggard (Prov. 26:13-16; 22:13), he knows better than God and godly counselors. When rebuked for his laziness, he offers this defense: "There is a lion in the road! A lion is in the open square!" (v. 13). Never mind that no one else has seen this imaginary lion. Never mind that other people have gone to work without being attacked. Never mind that lions don't usually spend their time on the open road or in the town square. Derek Kidner says that this man "will be the last to see his own features." As far as he is concerned, "he is not a shirker, but a realist (13); not self-indulgent, but below his best in the morning (14); his inertia is an objection to being hustled (15); his mental indolence a fine sticking to his guns (16)."[1]

Here we have a classic example of "overtalk" in the form of defensive, self-justifying speech. Regrettably, defensiveness and excuse making are frequently practiced in families today. Wives do it when their husbands suggest changes they would like their wives to make. Reasons for not changing abound: "I'd do that if you . . ." "With all the pressures I have on me . . ." "Since you don't give me the help I need . . ." "You never show appreciation, so . . ."

Husbands also practice defensiveness with their wives. A husband can make his wife feel like a bad person for even raising the issue. "You're unreasonable for wanting me to do what you're asking me to do. What about all the good things I do for you? Why do you always have to find fault?" "You're just too emotional. It's probably that time of the month again." "I think everything is fine the way it is. Why can't you ever be satisfied?" "Compared to the way John treats his wife, you should be happy." "How can you say I don't love you? I don't beat you! I have never been unfaithful. I try to provide for you. Why can't you get it through you're head that all I'm trying to do is . . ." Defensiveness! Self-justification! Destructiveness!

Takeover Speech

Takeover speech also qualifies as "overtalk." You're having a conversation and suddenly the other person interrupts: "Wait a minute, you were wrong about some of the details, and you missed some important facts. Let me fill in the gaps." He not only fills in the details but goes on to finish the story. He wants the privilege of giving the punchline and basking in the resultant laughter at what *he* has said. When that goes on constantly in husband-wife relationships, or parent-child relationships, it can be the soil in which resentment, bitterness, and frustration develop.

Motor-mouth Speech

Certainly non-stop or motor-mouth speech is a kind of "overtalk." Proverbs speaks of certain people who babble (Prov. 10:8, 10). Some people are just like a spring. Words pour forth from their mouths in a never-ending flow. For a short while it may be interesting and even amusing to have a motor-mouth in the family. But before long, inane conversation can become a source of irritation.

Scripture warns us of the danger of this kind of talk in two ways. It calls the person who practices it a "fool" (Prov. 10:8, 10).

Scripture also says that he "will be thrown down." Note that the text doesn't merely say that he will fall down; it says he "will be thrown down." Disaster, defeat, rejection, and humiliation will be his portion. These consequences may occur in any area of life: economic, occupational, emotional, spiritual, social, or familial.

When I think of these verses, a man I'll call "Jim" comes to mind. Jim and his wife came for counseling because they were experiencing severe marital conflict. Both were professing Christians, but they were fighting like cats and dogs. Actually Jim did most of the fighting—he was openly aggressive. His wife usually retreated, withdrawing passively on the outside, while standing firm on the inside. From the time they entered my office, Jim's mouth gushed with words. I never knew him to be silent. Not surprisingly, his wife was a very quiet person who simply sat there while Jim babbled on and on.

One day in a counseling session, I directed Jim's attention to these verses and asked him what he thought it meant to babble. At first, he was evasive, but finally gave a good description of what it meant. I then invited his interpretation of being "thrown down." Jim began to laugh. When I asked him why, he responded: "That's what has happened to me. I've been a babbling fool, and I've been thrown down. My marriage is a disaster. My wife has rejected me. She won't even read the Bible with me or pray with me. Our sex life is nonexistent. She treats me like I'm an enemy. My children don't care about me. Neither of them pays much attention to me or is interested in spiritual things. One has been on drugs and the other has no purpose or direction in life. That verse describes what has happened to me. I've been thrown down." And so it has happened with many others.

Badgering

"Overtalk" may take the form of badgering others, particularly in the home. Proverbs 17:9 may be describing this practice when it says, "He who repeats a matter separates intimate friends." Think of the person who gets on a topic and never gets off. He has one theme, and he badgers you about it repeatedly. Such a person thinks that persistent harassing is the way to get other people to agree. Initially that may seem to get results, but eventually it is very destructive. The conversational stone that this person rolls will come back on him (Prov. 26:27).

Situational "Overtalk"

One kind of "overtalk" to which I am most prone is what I call *"situational 'overtalk.'"* In general, I'm not a motor-mouth. Chitchat is something I have to make myself do. But there are certain topics in which I have done a lot of study and had a great deal of experience. Whenever these topics come up, I can very easily violate the biblical teaching that "a prudent man conceals knowledge, but the heart of fools proclaims folly" (Prov. 12:23).

Occasionally with my wife and children I may act imprudently by not keeping my knowledge to myself. What I'm saying may not be in error, but I "proclaim folly" in that I say too much or take too long to say it. The result is that I do not give my wife or children the opportunity to share their insights. I've either already said what they were going to say or my supposed expertise has intimidated them into a haven of silence. When I act this way, I am guilty of "overtalk." And if this were to happen on a regular basis, I would be hindering the personal growth of other family members and the development of good family relations.

Self-centered Speech

An abundance of self-centered speech is a common type of "overtalk." Proverbs 27:2 refers to this when it says, "Let another praise you, and not your own mouth; a stranger, and not your own lips." When you're involved in conversation with some people, the main topic of conversation revolves around themselves. They talk about their problems, their pains, their successes, their acquisitions, their victories, their training. Ninety-five percent of the conversation is "I and me" talk. Initially they may have some interesting stories to tell, and people may be attracted to them. But after a while others recognize how self-centered they are. Their relationships with others remain superficial and awkward. It is difficult to get close to someone who is wrapped up in himself. "It is not good to eat too much honey, nor is it honorable to seek one's own honor" (Prov. 25:27, NIV).

Reasons for "Overtalk"

Pride

Why do people become habituated to "overtalk"? One reason is pride. Excessive talk may reflect a desire to stand in the spotlight. Bragging, monopolizing conversations, and gossiping are ways of projecting self.

When someone listens carefully to another without interrupting or allowing his mind to drift, he manifests respect for the other person. Sometimes listening takes humility because the limelight is on someone else. Conversely, when a person dominates a conversation, it's as if he were saying: "I deserve to have everyone focus on me. I'm the only one who has anything worthwhile to say. I am so important, so knowledgeable, so interesting that I should do most, if not all, of the talking."

Selfishness

Where there is pride there is also selfishness. One "overtalker" I know is an expert at maneuvering all conversations in his family to fit his agenda. Though pretending to be interested in his wife's or children's point of view, in practice he either stifles what they have to say or brushes it aside as worthless. He is a vivid illustration of the fool who "does not delight in understanding, but only in revealing his own mind" (Prov. 18:2). His style of communication in the home is a flagrant violation of the scriptural admonition, "Do nothing from selfishness or empty conceit, but with humility of mind let each of you regard one another as more important than himself; do not merely look out for your own personal interests, but also for the interests of others" (Phil. 2:3, 4).

Fear of Silence

Some people "overtalk" because they are afraid of silence. They think that silence is bad, and therefore pauses in conversations make them anxious. They feel that it is their responsibility to keep the conversation going and that if they don't, people will think they're stupid.

They talk about whatever comes to their minds, regardless of whether it is of any substance. It may be a complaint about personal problems. They may grouse about the problems of others or of the world. Sometimes their "overtalk" takes the form of gossip. Generally their verbal meandering runs in a negative vein. They seem to be experts at digging up evil and finding fault (Prov. 16:27)—anything to relieve their social anxiety. Their incessant talking is a symptom of a deeper problem.

Loneliness

Lonely people frequently become "overtalkers." That was certainly true of Mary. Her relationship with her husband had always been superficial, though she desired genuine companionship with him. She wanted them to be co-heirs of grace in practice as well as in theory. But her husband showed no interest. He seemed apathetic about almost everything, including Mary. He went to work and came home, ate supper, watched television, and went to bed. The next day was the same routine.

Mary's dissatisfaction began early in their marriage. Wanting her husband to become her friend, she wondered how she could close the gap between them and overcome her loneliness. Mary tried to solve this problem with words. She talked at the dinner table, in the family room, when he was trying to watch television, when they were riding in the car. At first, her husband seemed to give her some attention. But soon he merely tolerated her continuous talking and tuned her out. Not knowing what else to do, Mary just turned up the volume in an unsuccessful attempt to overcome her loneliness.

Past Training or Habit

"Overtalkers" are often products of their past training. If one or both parents jabbered constantly, their child could become a babbler merely by following their example. It may never occur to him that he has formed a bad habit. Following his chief role models, his prattling has become second nature.

A habit is something we do unconsciously. Often many counselees are surprised when I point out habits such as "overtalking" in their behavior.

In one situation a wife and her children were being verbally abused by her husband. He constantly pressured them, seemingly wanting to make them clones of himself. Yet he could not understand why she wanted to take the children and leave. He gave illustration after illustration of how he had tried to be loving and considerate. He thought he was always willing to listen to his wife. He would seldom if ever do anything without her agreement. He couldn't comprehend why she felt that she and the children were being abused. He deeply loved them, and all he wanted, so he said, was to have a biblical home.

During our counseling sessions, I observed him practicing several forms of "overtalk," including defensive speech and badgering. He could justify everything he did that might appear unbiblical or self-ish. When a difference of opinion arose, he would plead for the opportunity to explain his position over and over in hopes that he would bring us around to his view. At times, he would manifest anger at being misunderstood. At other times, he would shed tears. Sometimes he would actually beg for agreement with his perspective. Though unquestionably an "overtalker," he was blind to his habit.

When I first pointed it out to him, he was incredulous. To help him to understand his problem, I had him tape and listen to several family conversations over a period of weeks. He finally became aware of what he was doing, acknowledged it, and agreed to change this destructive practice.

Not everyone who admits to being an "overtalker" recognizes how damaging that can be. This man did and was able to work on reversing the negative impact his habit had on his family.

Poor Listening

Poor listening may also precipitate "overtalk." The scenario played out in many homes is that a poor listener encourages other family members to nag. If a wife were sure her husband listened to her message the first time, she wouldn't need to repeat it. That doesn't excuse her nagging, because the Bible forbids such talk. But it does explain the tendency of one person to overcompensate for the other person's inattentiveness by piling up words. So, one way to deal with "overtalking" is to listen carefully the first time.

A Desire to Control Topics

Excessive talking may be used as a controlling mechanism. Some people think that if they allow you to talk, they lose control. You may introduce a subject they know nothing about or ask a question that makes them feel uncomfortable. To prevent that, they talk so much that no one else has a chance to take the conversation where they would rather not go. As long as they are at the conversational helm, they feel they are in safe waters and in control.

Perhaps a wife is afraid that her husband wants to talk about certain issues that she'd rather avoid—things like finances or sex or child discipline. She thinks that discussing them is too painful and will only cause more problems. When she fears one of these topics may come up, she seizes control of the conversation so that her husband can't introduce the dreaded subject. Her "overtalk" is a protective device, a diversion that helps her to control which issues she has to face.

Suggestions for Overcoming "Overtalk"

Because "overtalk" is a serious hindrance to building your family God's way, it is extremely important to take action to overcome it. Here are some practical suggestions for dealing with the problem.

1. *Evaluate whether you have a problem with "overtalk."* Review the different forms of "overtalk" previously discussed. Use the rating inventory found in the application section at the end of this chapter to assess your "overtalk" quotient. List the kinds of "overtalk" that you rate 0 or 1 or 2.

Then ask other people to evaluate you. In many instances you won't recognize that you are an "overtalker," but other people will. Ask your spouse or children if they think you "overtalk" in any of the ways delineated in this chapter. Insist that they be honest with you and not just say, "You're wonderful." If you really want to become a better Christian and a more productive individual, find some close friends who are really going to level with you and ask them. Remember, "Faithful are the wounds of a friend, but deceitful are the kisses of an enemy" (Prov. 27:6).

2. If you discover that there are ways in which you are guilty of overtalking, *make it a matter of prayer.* Pray with the psalmist: "Let the words of my mouth and the meditation of my heart be acceptable in Thy sight, O Lord, my rock and my Redeemer" (Ps. 19:14). "Set a guard, O Lord, over my mouth; keep watch over the door of my lips" (Ps. 141:3).

It is true, as James says, that "no one can tame the tongue" (James 3:8). But what no man can do, God can do. "Nothing is too difficult for Thee [God]" (Jer. 32:17). "The fruit of the Spirit is . . . self-control" (Gal. 5:22). "With God all things are possible" (Matt. 19:26). By his grace and through the power of the Holy Spirit, God who has redeemed you through the cross of Jesus Christ can help you to conquer the problems of "overtalk" and its underlying causes.

3. *Seek to identify the reasons behind your behavior.* As we have seen, "overtalk" is often a symptom of more significant issues. To overcome it, you must deal with it on more than a behavioral level. You must identify its cause.

4. When you have identified the cause of your overtalk, study the Scriptures to *discover God's way of resolving the underlying difficulty.* There is a biblical solution for any of the reasons behind your "overtalk." Remember, "No temptation [or situation or problem] has overtaken you but such as is common to man; and God is faithful, who will not allow you to be tempted beyond what you are able, but with the temptation will provide the way of escape . . ." (1 Cor. 10:13). In our union with Jesus Christ and in his precious promises (found in the Bible), God has given us *everything* we need for life and godliness (2 Pet. 1:3, 4). "Everything" certainly includes the ability to overcome "overtalk."

5. Select and *become familiar with Scripture that specifically deals with "overtalk"* and the reasons you practice it. Some of the Scripture quoted in this chapter would be very appropriate. You will find additional help in a Bible concordance or my book, *A Homework Manual for Biblical Living*, vol. 1 (Phillipsburg, N.J.: Presbyterian and Reformed, 1979). Memorize relevant Scripture; let it richly dwell in you (Col. 3:16). Call it to mind when you are tempted to "overtalk." God's Word has power (Heb. 4:12). It is able to keep us from sin and cleanse our way (Ps. 119:9, 11; John 15:3; 17:17).

6. Begin the day by *reviewing relevant Scripture*. Remind yourself of your purpose to be more prudent in your speech, and have check points throughout the day (lunch, dinner, bedtime) when you evaluate whether or not you have succeeded. If you have, thank God for his help and renew your commitment. If you haven't, ask God for his forgiveness and help, and renew your commitment.

7. *Make yourself accountable* to other family members (Heb. 3:12, 13). Ask them to pray for you and to inform you if they hear you practicing any forms of "overtalk." Perhaps you could work out a secret signal between you and your spouse to help you control your tongue in public.

8. *Persevere in following these suggestions* until you have put off the destructive practice of "overtalk" and have become trained in saying enough, but not too much, with other family members (1 Tim. 4:7; Heb. 5:14).

Study and Application Assignments

Do the assignments individually, then discuss your answers with your mate or your study group.

1. Study the following verses and note what each one has to say about "overtalk." Note the words that imply "overtalk." Note also the forms of "overtalk" described and their impact on others. Here are two examples:

   a. Job 11:2-4: "multitude of words," "talkative man"; defensive speech; encourages others to continue to attack.

   b. Job 19:2, 3: "How long," "These *ten times* you have insulted me"; badgering speech; hearer feels tormented, insulted, wronged, hurt, angry.

   c. Proverbs 11:13

   d. Proverbs 13:3

   e. Proverbs 15:2

   f. Proverbs 16:28

   g. Proverbs 20:19

h. Proverbs 25:14

i. Ecclesiastes 5:2, 3

j. Ecclesiastes 5:4-7

k. Ecclesiastes 10:14

l. Matthew 6:7

m. Ephesians 5:3

2. Reflect on the teaching of this chapter and answer these questions:

   a. What forms of "overtalk" are mentioned in this chapter?

   b. Are there other forms that you have observed? Describe them.

   c. What reasons for "overtalk" are mentioned in this chapter?

   d. Can you think of any other reasons?

   e. What do you think of the suggestions for overcoming "overtalk"? Would they be helpful? Can you make other suggestions?

3. Use the following inventory to determine how often you practice forms of "overtalk": 4 = never, 3 = seldom, 2 = sometimes, 1 = often, 0 = usually. Circle the number that best fits you.

   a. Monopolizing speech   43210
   b. Gossip   43210
   c. Defensive speech   43210
   d. Takeover speech   43210
   e. Motor-mouth speech   43210
   f. Badgering   43210
   g. Situational overtalk   43210
   h. Self-centered speech   43210
   i. Other_____   43210

   Total the number of 2s: ___ (need for some improvement).
   Total the number of 1s: ___ (need for more improvement).
   Total the number of 0s: ___ (need for major improvement).

4. Use the following inventory to evaluate any areas in which your family may practice overtalk: 1 = quantity is just right; 0 = quantity is too much.

   a. Spiritual issues, church, devotions, Bible
      truths, prayer, Christian service, etc.   1 0
   b. Facts, information   1 0
   c. Ideas, opinions   1 0
   d. Feelings   1 0

e. Desires, concerns, interests	1 0
f. Plans, goals	1 0
g. Dreams, aspirations	1 0
h. Finances, material things, purchases, savings, investments	1 0
i. Work, school	1 0
j. Sexual matters, desires, likes, dislikes	1 0
k. Friends	1 0
l. Recreation, sports, vacations, relaxation	1 0
m. Problems, failures	1 0
n. Joys, victories, successes	1 0
o. What you read, study, learn, hear, see	1 0
p. Current events, politics	1 0
q. Other _____	1 0

Note items for which you think there is too much talk. Discuss with your mate and family whether or not they agree, and what can be done to improve in these areas.

5. Reflect on the reasons for "overtalk" that were mentioned and, if you have any problem on this matter, seek to identify the reason(s) behind your "overtalk."

	Yes/ No/ Maybe
a. Pride	___ ___ ___
b. Selfishness	___ ___ ___
c. Fear or anxiety	___ ___ ___
d. Loneliness	___ ___ ___
e. Past training or habit	___ ___ ___
f. Poor listening	___ ___ ___
g. A desire to control topics	___ ___ ___
h. Other _____	___ ___ ___

6. If you have identified the forms of "overtalk" to which you are prone and the reasons behind this practice, discuss with your mate and family how you will implement the suggestions for overcoming them. Add anything you think would be helpful, and then follow through on them.

Notes
   [1]Derek Kidner, *The Proverbs* (Downers Grove, Ill.: InterVarsity Press, 1972), p. 163.

8

Circuit Jammers to Family Communication

"You must be more brilliant than Einstein," said the student to his professor one day after class. Amazed and flattered, the professor inquired, "Why do you say that?" "Well," the student explained, "They say only eight people in the world could understand Einstein. But nobody can understand you!"

Talking and communicating are not necessarily the same thing, as that professor found out. On a number of occasions I have tried to telephone someone but could not get through because the circuits were jammed. Something was happening on the line that made it impossible to complete my call. Had I nevertheless sat there and talked into my telephone for several hours, no one would have been the better for it. The message wasn't reaching the person for whom it was intended.

Keep Those Circuits Open!

It is very common for the circuits to become jammed in family communication. Dysfunctional families may not be at a loss for verbiage. Messages are being sent, but family members are not receiving and understanding them. Nor are words being used to edify, encourage, and bring family members into closer harmony (Eph. 4:25, 29). The circuits of communication must be unjammed if these families are to function biblically.

What causes jammed communication circuits in the home? A

disparity between verbal and nonverbal communication is one cause (see chapters 4 and 5). "Overtalk" as described in chapter 7 is a second culprit. But there are additional communication blockers, and the Bible will help us to understand what they are.

Ephesians 4:25-30 describes some of the "bugs" that kill effective family communication.

> Therefore, laying aside falsehood, speak truth, each one of you, with his neighbor, for we are members of one another. Be angry, and yet do not sin; do not let the sun go down on your anger, and do not give the devil an opportunity. . . . Let no unwholesome word proceed from your mouth, but only such a word as is good for edification according to the need of the moment, that it may give grace to those who hear. And do not grieve the Holy Spirit of God, by whom you were sealed for the day of redemption.

Ephesians 1-3 presents some of the great doctrines of the Christian faith, particularly what God has done for believers through Jesus Christ. The incredible privileges that Christians have and their wealth because of their union with Jesus Christ are the central message of these three chapters.

The key verse of this section is Ephesians 1:3, where Paul says, "Blessed be the God and Father of our Lord Jesus Christ, who has blessed us with every spiritual blessing in the heavenly places in Christ." Here Paul announces the theme and purpose of this portion of Scripture. The theme? The fantastic blessings we have in Christ. The purpose? That we might be stimulated to appreciate, and praise God for these blessings.

At the beginning of chapter 4, Paul changes his emphasis from what God has done to what we should do in response. He turns from his focus on our relationship with God to a discussion of our relationship with people. Having told us about our privileges and resources in Christ (Eph. 1-3), Paul then describes the impact that should have on our daily lives (Eph. 4-6). The way he begins this segment is extremely important: "I, therefore . . . entreat you to walk in a manner worthy of the calling with which you have been called" (Eph. 4:1).

The word "therefore" informs us that whatever Paul is going to exhort us to do is based upon what he has just told us. Because of our blessings in Christ, we can and should live our lives in a "worthy manner." The specifics of that "worthy manner" are delineated in Ephesians 4-6. Instructions about how to relate to other people form the bulk of this section, with effective communication given star billing in Ephesians 4:25-30. Two broad categories of circuit-jamming speech are highlighted in this passage: falsehood and unwholesome talk.

Falsehood

In verse 25 we are told that falsehood will block communication in your family. Most parents dismiss this warning, saying: "I don't lie to other family members. Maybe the children do, but not I." But the Bible says, "The heart is deceitful above all things and beyond cure" (Jer. 17:9, NIV). "Even from birth the wicked go astray; from the womb they are wayward and speak lies" (Ps. 58:3, NIV). "For from within, out of men's hearts, come evil thoughts,... deceit..." (Mark 7:21, 22).

It would be nice if these verses only applied to a select few, but the context of each passage forbids that. The Bible indicates that *all* of us practice lying. We all have deceitful and wayward hearts that have gone astray from birth and spoken lies. Some of us are more deceitful than others, but none of us has ever been absolutely honest. We didn't have to be taught to lie. It came naturally. That's why there are so many exhortations in the Bible about the seriousness of dishonesty.

Blatant Lying

Falsehood may be practiced in several ways. The most familiar form is blatant lying. Family members say, "Yes, I'll do it," but don't; "I didn't do that," but they actually did; "I didn't mean it the way you're taking it," when they did mean it that way; "I have no idea what happened to it," when they do know, but would rather not say; "I was only kidding," when they meant every word; "I'm sorry I forgot to do what you asked me to," when they aren't sorry and they didn't merely forget.

Fear moved Abraham to lie to Pharaoh about his relationship with his wife (Gen. 12:10-20). The same was true of Abraham's son Isaac (Gen. 26:1-11). Greed and covetousness motivated Jacob to deceive his blind father to steal the birthright from his brother Esau (Gen. 27). Envy and bitterness prompted Joseph's brothers to lie when they told their father that a wild animal must have killed their brother (Gen. 37).

These biblical examples demonstrate five things about lying: (1) it is a common practice; (2) even godly people will be tempted to lie; (3) we should take the exhortation to guard against lying seriously; (4) other family members become aware of lies; and (5) lying causes personal and family trouble.

Continuous or unconfessed lying breaks communication and hurts relationships. Consider the example of Jacob. Genesis 27-31 relates several instances where Jacob's greed led him to deceive his family. There is no indication that Jacob ever asked God or his family for forgiveness. The result? Jacob had to leave his home. He never saw his parents again. His relationship with his brother was destroyed for many years. His relationship with his father-in-law Laban became hostile to the point that when they parted, Laban threatened his life if he ever returned.

Blatant lying took its toll on Jacob's family relationships. It is no different today. As a pastoral counselor I could tell you of case after case in which blatant lying wreaked havoc in the home. I think of one husband who lost all confidence in his wife because of her continuous lying. The couple would discuss a family matter, and she would agree to what the husband thought was a mutually accepted decision. But when he wasn't around, she would do the opposite of what they had decided. When the husband would find out, he would feel deceived and betrayed. After years of this he felt trapped married to a wife he could not trust. She had sown blatant lying and reaped a harvest of bitterness, resentment, and distrust.

Lethal Exaggeration

Exaggeration is a more subtle, but equally lethal form of lying. It occurs when we blow things out of proportion. Sometimes we exaggerate about a person's behavior. "You never want to do what

I want to do!" "You're always late!" "You're always too tired!" "You're never ready on time!" "You yell all the time!" "I always have to clean up after you!" "You never are willing to face issues!" "You have an excuse for everything!" "I can never count on you!" "You say you'll change, but you never do!" "Nothing ever suits you!" "You always get upset!" "You'll never learn!"

Sometimes we exaggerate concerning our own conduct. "I never do anything like that!" "Nothing ever upsets me!" "I'm always in a good mood!" "I help you all the time!" "I give in to you all the time!" "Nothing could be further from the truth about me!"

Words such as "always," "never," "nothing," "totally," "absolutely," and "all the time" serve as red flags, warning us of possible overstatement. It's rarely true that someone "always" commits a certain offense or "never" performs a particular good deed. But it is no exaggeration to say that family relationships are hurt by such exaggerations. Exaggerated statements are often spoken out of exasperation and come across as attacks or defensiveness. No one enjoys being labeled negatively or hearing another overstate his own virtues. As a result exaggeration encourages people to become defensive or suspicious of the speaker. Although intended to get the listener's attention, exaggeration usually fosters disbelief or disregard for what is said. "Overkill" words make it obvious that the speaker is departing from the truth. The listener begins to feel abused and mistreated, having lost confidence in the speaker and his words. Frequent and uncorrected exaggeration sabotages family relationships by producing the weeds of suspicion, resentment, resistance, withdrawal, counterattacks, and faultfinding.

Misrepresentation

Misrepresentation, a close cousin to exaggeration, is part of the falsehood family. Perhaps there is no more common form of lying than when the facts about a person and his behavior are rearranged. The truth is so twisted and distorted by additions or omissions or slanting of facts that the result bears little resemblance to reality.

In one "Hagar the Horrible" comic strip, Hagar went to his doctor for a physical exam. After examining him, the doctor said:

"You're fat and flabby. For a man your age, I'm amazed at the shape you're in." When he went home, and his wife asked what the doctor said, Hagar deceitfully replied, "For a man my age, he was amazed at the shape I'm in."

Hagar misrepresented what the doctor said by taking his words out of context. He omitted what was unmistakably negative and probably quoted the rest in an upbeat manner so as to turn the doctor's negative evaluation into a positive one.

Like Hagar, many of us misrepresent the facts about ourselves in order to curry favor, win sympathy, save face, escape criticism, and exalt or protect ourselves. Initially, misrepresenting our achievements, abilities, and experiences, or our failures, weaknesses, and defeats, may seem profitable. Eventually, however, the truth becomes known, and our falsifications damage our family relationships.

Equally common and serious is the practice of misrepresenting others. Job experienced misrepresentation from his so-called friends. They were sure that there were deep, dark, secret sins in Job's life for which he was being punished. Consequently they made false accusations against him.

The apostle Paul encountered the same kind of treatment. Out of jealousy and hostility people often tried to discredit him and his gospel. They spread rumors about his conduct. They twisted what he said and misconstrued his motives for doing good. Misrepresentation followed him throughout his ministry (1 Cor. 4:9-13; 2 Cor. 1:13-24; 2 Cor. 12:11-19; 1 Thess. 2:1-11).

Imagine, for example, how easy it would be to distort the words of Paul in Ephesians 4:28: "Let him who steals steal no longer; but rather let him labor, performing with his own hands what is good, in order that he may have something to share with him who has need." By simply omitting one phrase and changing one punctuation mark, Paul's exhortation could be completely misrepresented to read, "Let him who steals steal, no longer performing with his own hands what is good. . . ." That is all it would take to stand Paul's message about selfless giving on its head.

Each of us has also known the pain of being misrepresented. What we say is misquoted or understated or overstated, or given a different tone or inflection or nuance. Some of this distortion takes place within our own families. As Jesus warned us, there are times when a person is mistreated by members of his own household (Matt. 10:36). What's more, when we're hurt by other people, we tend in turn to misrepresent their words and motives, causing greater dissension in the home.

When people fear they will be misrepresented, they avoid discussing issues on which they don't want to be misquoted. Reluctant to supply ammunition that will be used against them, they express themselves sparingly and on a superficial level. It's not difficult to understand why misrepresentation undermines effective family communication.

Unwholesome Talk

A second broad category of circuit-jamming speech is mentioned in Ephesians 4:29. Paul says, "Let no unwholesome word proceed from your mouth." Unwholesome talk, like falsehood, must be expunged from our conversation.

The Greek word translated "unwholesome" was used in a variety of ways. Unwholesome fruit was rotten fruit—offensive to the smell, sight, and touch, and possibly harmful if eaten. A ravaging disease was called an unwholesome disease. The Greek translation of the Old Testament uses this word to describe the disease that caused Job's flesh to waste away (Job 33:21). Matthew 13:48 employs it when bad or unwholesome fish are contrasted with good fish, either because the unwholesome fish were diseased or because they were not nutritious.

Applying this to the "unwholesome" talk of Ephesians 4:29, we see that the speech in this category covers a wide spectrum. It includes any talk that is unhealthy, unproductive, corrupt, harmful, poisonous, or destructive. Speech that can be characterized by any of these terms must be considered a circuit jammer and laid aside.

Sidetracking

Included under the category of unproductive speech would be what I call "sidetracking." It happens when, in the course of conversation, no one issue is thoroughly discussed. The subject constantly changes without anything being brought to a resolution. In sidetracking, many issues are spilled onto the table, but you come away from such a conversation feeling overwhelmed because nothing constructive is settled.

I remember counseling one lady who complained about her husband's unwillingness to communicate. According to her, all the problems in their marriage (and they were many) were his fault. "I'm not satisfied with the depth of our relationship," she said. "I want more out of life and our marriage than I'm now experiencing. But my husband isn't interested in facing issues and improving our marriage. I just can't get him to talk about important matters. All he wants to do is sit around and watch television."

Problems are rarely as one-sided as she made them out to be, and so I tried to unpack some of her complaints and give her direction in responding appropriately. After a few sessions, I had the frustrating sense that we were going nowhere. Then I realized what was happening.

When she came for her weekly counseling session, she would begin by saying: "Let me tell you what happened this week. We just have to talk about some things." Then she would set off on a topic, and we would discuss it as I tried to help her to find God's perspective on it. But before we would settle on a biblical solution, she would head off on another subject. This woman was a master at sidetracking. She was constantly hopping from one issue to the next without allowing a thorough discussion of any. A lot of fires had been started, but none had been put out.

I wondered if her sidetracking explained her husband's unwillingness to discuss matters with her. So I explained to her what I observed in our counseling and how I had felt when it happened. More than that, I asked her if it would be all right to tape our sessions so that she could hear what she was doing. She agreed and followed through.

This exercise proved an eye-opener for her. After listening to the first tape, she came back saying: "I didn't like what I heard. I've always thought of myself as being very considerate and open-minded.

What I heard was an opinionated, close-minded person who was rude and overbearing." Through this she gained increased self-awareness about how her sidetracking jammed the circuits of communication.

We agreed on some conversational ground rules for our sessions, which I hoped would carry over to her communication at home. We made a list of topics to be discussed, decided on the order in which to consider them, and started working on them one by one. When she would slip back into her old habit of sidetracking, I would call it to her attention and refuse to allow her to change subjects before we had sufficiently considered the topic at hand. Slowly but surely her compulsion to ramble decreased, as did the frustration and confusion from lighting fires that were never extinguished.

In time her husband, who had refused to come for counseling, willingly joined us. He had noticed the changes in his wife and her communication style. They generated in him a willingness to work at improving their relationship.

Verbal Slamming

In the game of Ping-Pong, slamming the ball toward your opponent is a favorite tactic. Your opponent often must back up to return the ball as it careens off the table. Slamming drives Ping-Pong players farther apart. Another strategy that has the opposite effect is softly dribbling the ball over the net. To return the ball, a player must move closer to his opponent.

The slam may be a legitimate strategy for the sport of Ping-Pong. But when it comes to interpersonal communication, "slamming" is a form of unwholesome speech that must be laid aside. Hurling harsh and cutting words at family members will surely distance them from you, both spatially and emotionally. Scripture encourages us to become experts at the "dribble" technique. Dribbling soft, gentle, respectful words to people will draw them closer to you. Indeed, when it comes to interpersonal relationships, "a gentle answer turns away wrath, but a harsh word stirs up anger" (Prov. 15:1).

Cancellation Speech

Cancellation speech is a form of unwholesome communication. It occurs when something is said in one breath and taken back (cancelled) with the next. For example: "That was a good meal. Why don't you cook that well more often?" "I'm glad to see that you got A's in English and history, but why did you get those two B's and two C's in the other subjects?" "I really appreciate the way you mowed the lawn this time. I just wish you'd do it that way more often." "Thanks for calling me when you were going to be late. I just can't understand why you don't do that all the time." "Sure you're honest and hard-working and loyal, but you are so stupid and boring and uninteresting."

Some time ago a man known as an outstanding Bible teacher and Christian leader took one of our courses at the Christian Counseling and Educational Foundation. Upon completing the course, he wrote the instructor a letter stating that he appreciated the course because it was very biblical, practical, and filled with good information. He concluded by adding that he hadn't learned anything new, but still found the course to be a very helpful reminder of things he already knew.

The effort this man made to write a letter is commendable, but the last part of his note raised some questions. Why did he practice cancellation speech? Did he add the phrase about not learning anything new because he didn't want the instructor to become proud? Or did he not want to admit he could possibly have learned anything from the teacher? Did he want the teacher to think that he already knew it all?

Cancellation speech often manifests *pride* intent on exalting self by keeping others in their place—a lower place. Pride is what inhibits us from simply expressing appreciation for someone else's ministry without some kind of a disclaimer. Pride causes us to let others know that whatever good ideas they have, we had them long before they did—or at least without their aid. Pride causes us to want to correct or find fault with the suggestions of other people.

Pride often leads us to say things like: "That's a good idea. In fact, I was thinking the same thing three months ago." "You're on the right track, but I have several ideas that would make it much better..." "I can understand why you might think that way, but here are some reasons why what you're saying isn't true." "What he said was pretty good, but if you knew what I know about him, you wouldn't be as impressed."

Scripture indicates that pride brings dishonor and disrupts relationships (Prov. 11:2; 13:10). It may dishonor others openly or in more subtle ways, perhaps by withholding appreciation from others by seldom or never saying "thank you." Or it may express itself through cancellation speech. Theoretically the person who engages in this practice can never be accused of not saying "thank you." He may pride himself in that he has said something good about another person, not realizing that in the next breath he has nullified his positive comment. He can't comprehend why anyone would think he is unappreciative.

Gunpowder Speech

Proverbs 18:6 describes a very serious kind of unwholesome talk, which I call "gunpowder speech": "A fool's lips bring him strife, and his mouth invites a beating" (NIV). When some people shoot off their mouths, it's all you can to do to keep from firing back, verbally if not physically. Their explosive speech invites a beating, figuratively or literally.

On one occasion, I complimented a counselee on the good job she did in filling out her Personal Data Inventory form. She responded, "Well, wasn't that what everybody is supposed to do?" POW! Lord, give me grace! I outwardly ignored her provocative response and continued to read her form. Her answers indicated that she read her Bible and prayed often. I commented on that and added, "That's great!" to which she replied, "Well, isn't that what every Christian is supposed to do?" POW! Another flash of hostility. Then I found out that she memorized a lot of Scripture. I praised her for that and she retorted, "Well, isn't every Christian supposed to memorize Scripture?" It didn't matter what I said. She wanted to do battle, and even words of commendation set her off.

This woman's mouth was inviting a beating. I could understand why she didn't have any friends, why she felt lonely and alienated from people, and why she had problems with members of her family. Her gunpowder speech provoked and escalated conflicts, leading to defeat in her life.

Ventriloquistic Speech

When parents and their children come for counseling, I ask the children questions directly. Even though I look to them to answer, I sometimes hear a voice coming from the other side of the room. Mom or Dad is answering for them. Or I'll ask a husband a question and his wife will answer. Or when he answers the wife will say, "What he meant was . . ." If that's what he meant, then let him tell me!

Ventriloquistic speech takes over for the other person. It's like hogging the ball in a game of basketball. A dominant player may think he's the only one who can score, and so he refuses to pass the ball. The other players become resentful and may even give up trying to play. They may think: "What's the use? He wants to be the star. Let him be a one-man team." In family relationships, speaking for the other person has the same effect.

Final-Word Speech

Some speakers project the attitude that once they have spoken on a subject, nothing more can be added; the ultimate has been spoken. They're like "Mr. Talkative" in *Pilgrim's Progress*, who spoke at great length on almost any subject. Impressed with himself, he expected others would respond to him the same way. Instead they found him to be a boring windbag and a pompous, shallow person.

One woman thought she knew exactly what was right for her husband and daughter. She considered herself the family oracle. She knew the topics about which her daughter should write term papers. She knew what her daughter should do with her life. She knew how her husband should conduct his business. She knew what was wrong in the church and in the world and what ought to be done about it. She also knew why her husband and daughter had problems listening and relating to her: they were worldly, unspiritual, lacking in godliness. In reality, they were tired of being treated like morons by someone who wanted to do their thinking for them. Her final-word style of communicating had created an immense barrier between her and her family.

Excessive Negative Talk

Some people constantly complain and find fault. They seldom affirm or talk about positive virtues of other people. They rarely acknowledge the good things happening in the world or in the church or in their family. They are experts at excessive negative talk.

The gloom and doom that pours from the mouths of these people fosters a depressing atmosphere in the family. Home becomes a place where spirits are weighed down rather than lifted, where heaviness rather than happiness prevails—a place people want to avoid.

Mind-Reading Speech

Speculating about another person's thoughts or motives is a very common type of unwholesome speech. Jane hears Mark say something and says: "I know what you meant by that, and it isn't what you want me to think. I want you to know that I don't like it one bit."

Mark responds, "What do you think I meant?"

"You meant. . . ."

"No, that's not what I meant. I really meant. . . ."

"You can't fool me. I've lived with you too long and I know you too well. What you meant is. . . . Come on, admit that this is what is going on."

This conversation may seem far-fetched. But what I've described could well be a common occurrence in your family. Perhaps you are the victim or the perpetrator of such behavior.

Many people consider mind-reading to be a harmless practice. Usually, they're the ones doing the mind-reading! When the shoe is on the other foot and they're being told dogmatically what is on their minds, then they see it differently.

Verbal Manipulation

Personal growth and positive family relationships may also be impaired by verbal attempts to control, manipulate, or punish people. One twenty-nine-year-old lady came for counseling with some very serious personal and family problems. She had tried to commit suicide on numerous occasions. Initially her presentation problem was her marriage relationship. It soon became evident that her difficulties involved more than her relationship with her husband. Data gathering revealed that her mother manipulated and punished her by saying things like: "You'll be the death of me yet." "I wish you had never been born; I never wanted you anyway." "You're just no good."

When she was a little girl, those words would ring in her ears as she crept into bed. Fear, hurt, and shame interfered with sleep because she thought her mother might die during the night, and it would be all her fault. She'd lie awake listening to her mother's breathing. Finally, she reached the point where she just wished her mother *would* die. She thought that would end her agony. "I would lie in my bed and picture my mother stretched out in a coffin."

Imagine the impact this woman's manipulative, punishing words had on that child! Intended to make her daughter conform to her expectations this woman's perverse words crushed the girl (Prov. 15:4) and destroyed their relationship.

Double-Bind Speech

Speech that puts people in a "catch twenty-two" situation is a widely practiced circuit jammer. Our words may create a double bind, sending forth two conflicting messages so that no matter what family members do, they are at fault.

I saw an illustration of this in the comic strip "Blondie." Dagwood, while on the telephone with Herb, turns to Blondie and says, "Herb wants me to go shoot some pool." Blondie replies, "If you don't mind leaving me here all by myself and if your own conscience will let you go, then I certainly will." And so Dagwood responds to Herb, "She said yes, but somehow it came out no." Dagwood was experiencing double-bind speech—he was getting two conflicting messages.

In one of our counselor training institutes, I noticed a sign on one of the more comfortable seats about ten minutes before the class was to begin: "This seat is reserved for Introduction to Biblical Counseling tonight from 6:00 to 9:30 p.m. All squatters will be shot. This means you. So scram." At the bottom of the sign this note was added: "P.S. I love you."

That's double-bind speech! We slap people with one sentence and then turn around and cuddle them with the next. The result is often confusion, frustration, and resentment.

Cotton-Candy Speech

When eaten in moderation, cotton candy may not be detrimental to your health. But woe to the person who makes it his main diet! Cotton candy simply will not build a strong body. It lacks the vitamins and minerals necessary for good health. People who depend on it will eventually die of starvation.

Many families are weak and frail because the main item on the communication menu is cotton candy speech. Conversations in these homes are usually superficial, lacking depth and substance. Surface talk, frivolous joking, and teasing form the bulk of the family's interactions. Because serious issues, painful and perplexing matters, and ultimate concerns are seldom discussed, the family relationships remain on a very shallow level.

Excessive Heavyweight Speech

The opposite must also be avoided. Some people are very serious-minded, deploring chit-chat as a horrible waste of time. They want to turn every conversation into a discussion of deep theological topics, problems, weighty subjects, and ultimate concerns. To them, laughing, kidding, talking about sports, or other fun diversions are of little or no value.

Certainly serious issues need to be discussed, problems should be confronted, and Bible truths should be studied and shared. But these people forget that God has given us all things richly to enjoy (1 Tim 6:17). Life is more than cotton candy, but it's also more than problems and perplexities. Some lighter fare is legitimate and even beneficial.

Living with a "heavyweight talker" can be a trying experience. Other family members may see the importance of talking about problems or exploring weighty theological issues, but they get tired of doing it continuously. They want to lighten up, to relax and smell the roses. They want to laugh and allow their minds to dwell on the things that are lovely and excellent (Phil. 4:8). They believe that everything God has created is good and is to be received and enjoyed with gratitude (1 Tim. 4:4).

When I encounter a situation in which "heavyweight talking" is hindering relationships in the home, I suggest that the family reserve a daily period for talking about deeper issues. I instruct them to limit their discussion of problems or other weighty issues to a specific length of time. For the rest of the day they are to avoid this kind of speech. Otherwise the whole of their lives and relationships become problematic.

I also ask them to do their "heavyweight talking" in a certain place. If they talk about problems in the car and problems in the bedroom and problems in the dining room and problems in the kitchen, it's going to take the fun out of life. Every family needs to maintain a proper balance between the heavier and lighter forms of conversation.

Hasty, Knee-Jerk Speech

A quick response is usually an unwise one and represents another form of unwholesome talk. The Bible warns us about this kind of behavior: "Do you see a man who is hasty in his words? There is more hope for a fool than for him" (Prov. 29:20). "It is a trap for a man to dedicate something rashly and only later to consider his vows" (Prov. 20:25, NIV). "Be quick to hear, slow to speak" (James 1:19). "Do not be quick with your mouth" (Eccl. 5:2, NIV).

King Saul exemplifies the destructive power of hasty speech. On one occasion his son Jonathan made a comment at the dinner table about his friend David that Saul didn't appreciate. "Saul's anger flared up at Jonathan and he said to him, 'You son of a perverse and rebellious woman! Don't I know that you have sided with the son of Jesse to your own shame.' . . . Jonathan got up from the table in fierce anger . . . he did not eat, because he was grieved at his father's shameful treatment . . ." (1 Sam. 20:30, 34, NIV).

It's evident from the context of 1 Samuel that the relationship between Saul and Jonathan was a strained one. Many factors probably entered into this estrangement, but it is reasonable to think that one of the primary factors was Saul's angry, hasty, knee-jerk way of talking. Words that are spoken in haste are seldom profitable. Frequently, like Saul's words, they are extremely destructive.

Do you want to build your family God's way? Take these circuit jammers seriously. On the surface they may seem innocent and harmless. But they aren't! They are lethal. To build your family God's way, I urge you to seek his help to identify and eliminate all forms of unwholesome speech from your family interactions.

Study and Application Assignments

Complete the assignments individually, then discuss your answers with your mate or your study group.

1. Study the following verses and note what each of them has to say about "communication bugs" (circuit jammers). Identify the circuit jammer mentioned and its impact on family relationships.

   a. Ephesians 4: 31

   b. Proverbs 12:18

   c. Proverbs 11:19

   d. Proverbs 16:27

   e. Proverbs 18:21

   f. Proverbs 17:9

   g. Proverbs 10:18

   h. Proverbs 13:3

i. Proverbs 15:1

j. Proverbs 16:28

k. Proverbs 18:7

l. Proverbs 22:14

m. Proverbs 24:28, 29

n. Proverbs 25:9, 10

o. Proverbs 25:24

p. Proverbs 26:18, 19

q. Proverbs 27:2

r. Proverbs 28:23, 24

s. Proverbs 29:20

t. Matthew 5:21-23

u. Matthew 5:33-37

v. James 3:1-12

w. James 4:11

x. James 5:9

y. James 5:12

2. Take the following Circuit Jammer Inventory. Some of these "jammers" were mentioned in the chapter, others were not. Evaluate yourself and other family members on each of the items mentioned. Use the rating scale: never do this (= 4), seldom do this (= 3), sometimes do this (= 2), often do this (= 1), usually do this (= 0). Be honest about your ratings. Make this a learning experience.

a. Lying	4 3 2 1 0
(1) Blatant	4 3 2 1 0
(2) Exaggeration	4 3 2 1 0
(3) Misrepresentation	4 3 2 1 0
b. Sidetracking	4 3 2 1 0
c. Verbal slamming	4 3 2 1 0
d. Abusive, mocking speech	4 3 2 1 0
e. Cancellation speech	4 3 2 1 0
f. Gunpowder speech	4 3 2 1 0
g. Ventriloquistic speech	4 3 2 1 0
h. Final-word speech	4 3 2 1 0
i. Excessive negative talk	4 3 2 1 0

j. Mind-reading speech	4 3 2 1 0
k. Overpowering speech (loud, forceful, pushy)	4 3 2 1 0
l. Manipulative, punitive speech	4 3 2 1 0
m. Double-bind speech	4 3 2 1 0
n. Disregarding speech (failure to acknowledge the other person's contributions)	4 3 2 1 0
o. Emotional, unrestrained talk (angry, dramatic, overreactive)	4 3 2 1 0
p. Disjointed speech (no connection to what is being discussed, out of place for circumstances)	4 3 2 1 0
q. Picayune speech (making big deals out of insignificant things)	4 3 2 1 0
r. Excessive cotton-candy speech	4 3 2 1 0
s. Excessive heavyweight, problem-oriented speech	4 3 2 1 0
t. Placating, insincere speech	4 3 2 1 0
u. Hasty, knee-jerk speech	4 3 2 1 0
v. Blameshifting, defensive speech	4 3 2 1 0
w. Ungodly, speech (saying things that are contrary to the Bible or that the Bible would not have us talk about)	4 3 2 1 0
x. Evasive talk (refusal to talk about issues directly, misleading people)	4 3 2 1 0
y. Profane, vulgar speech	4 3 2 1 0
z. Sarcastic speech (put-downs, cutting speech)	4 3 2 1 0

3. Note the "communication bugs" on which you scored yourself or other family members 0, 1, or 2. Pray about and plan what you can do to improve.

4. Read the following sentences and determine which of the twenty-six circuit jammers listed under assignment 2 they illustrate. Letter "a" is a sample of how to do this assignment.

a. You make me sick. c, d, f, k, l, o

b. I hope you get what you deserve._____

c. I don't really care what you think._____

d. You're going to be sorry._____

e. You are such a nit-wit, a real nincompoop._____

f. Why don't you just shut up!_____

g. This time, I'm going to get even._____

h. Just be quiet and let me tell you what you should do. I don't need to hear any more._____

i. Why in the world would you ever do something like that! _____

j. If you were a real woman [or man], you . . ._____

k. I know I promised to do it, but . . ._____

l. Anybody knows it's not the way you say it is._____

m. After what you've done, you expect me to love you?_____

n. I know why you did that!_____

o. I don't want to hear about your problems. I have enough of my own._____

p. You never care what I think._____

q. No one else can understand it or do it as well as I._____

r. You're never satisfied. _____

s. You're the one who always causes problems._____

t. Why don't you get off your high horse! _____

u. So I lied. Don't make such a big deal out of it._____

v. I know I shouldn't have done it, but . . . _____

w. Why can't you ever get anything right?_____

y. You'd never believe what I heard about Sally today. She . . . _____

y. Okay, have it your way. I'm the one who always gives in._____

z. You should have known I didn't really mean it. Anybody knows I was only kidding. You just take things too seriously._____

5. Go back over the list in number 4 and circle the letter before statements similar to ones you have made. Put a check by the statements that sound like things you have heard other family members say. Discuss the impact of such statements on you, your relationships, and others. Pray and work on eliminating such statements from your conversation.

9

To Tell the Truth

"Sticks and stones may break your bones, but words will never hurt you." This well-known proverb is one of the biggest lies ever foisted on the human race. According to Scripture, words can destroy neighbors (Prov. 11:9), tear down cities (Prov. 11:11), kill people (Prov. 12:6), ruin lives (Prov. 13:3), stir up anger (Prov. 15:1), and encourage despair and depression (Prov. 15:4). "The tongue is a fire, the very world of iniquity; the tongue ... defiles the entire body, and sets on fire the course of our life, and is set on fire by hell. . . . it is a restless evil and full of deadly poison" (James 3:6, 8).

Mankind has never invented an instrument with more destructive power than the human tongue. But that is only half the story. That same tongue can be an enormously positive, constructive force in your family life. Words can build up people (Prov. 18:21), bring blessing to an entire city (Prov. 11:11), relieve anxiety (Prov. 12:25), produce joy and satisfaction (Prov. 12:14), bring comfort and encouragement (1 Thess. 4:18), diminish anger and strife (Prov. 15:1), and bring delight and pleasure to God (Eph. 4:30; Mal. 3:16). "A soothing tongue is a tree of life" (Prov. 15:4); " . . . the tongue of the wise brings healing" (Prov. 12:18).

Several facts about the importance and power of verbal communication are delineated in Ephesians 4:25: "Each of you must . . . speak . . . to his neighbor, for we are all members of one body" (NIV) (1) We are commanded to *speak*. Communication is an obligation. Our Lord has told us to talk to one another. (2) *Each one of us* is commanded to speak. God wants every one of us to practice effective communication. No one is excused. Refusal to communicate is disobedience. (3) We are to speak each one of us *to his neighbor.* In this passage, the neighbor whom Paul has especially in mind is a fellow Christian. A neighbor, however, according to the broader context of Scripture, is anyone near us, any fellow human being with whom we are in contact (Luke 10:29-37). *Neighbors (husbands, wives, parents, children) should talk to one another.* (4) We are to speak to one another *because we are all members of one body,* or as the New American Standard Bible puts it, "we are members of one another." As fellow Christians, we have become intimately related to one another, parts of Christ's body (Eph. 4:16; 1 Cor. 12:13). Charles Hodge explains, "As it would be unnatural, absurd, frustrating and injurious for the hand not to communicate effectively with the foot, or the eye with the ear, so there is a violation of the very law of our union with each other when Christians do not communicate with one another."[1]

If the human body is to function as a unit, every part of the body needs to know what the other parts are going to do. If, for example, my head wants me to get up, but doesn't tell the rest of the body what it desires, I won't go anywhere. Families that fail to speak to one another experience the same results. Building your family God's way requires an adequate amount of the right kind of speech between family members. The alternative to talking to one another in an unwholesome, destructive way is not being silent, but speaking what is good and beneficial (Eph. 4:25, 29).

How the saying, "Sticks and stones may break your bones, but words will never hurt you" ever originated, I'm not sure. I have an idea it was conceived by someone who wanted to excuse his own irresponsible words. It certainly wasn't coined by someone who accepts God's perspective on speech or by anyone on the receiving end of careless, unwholesome talk. The truth is that sticks and stones can break your bones, but words can break your heart.

Paul's admonition to "let no unwholesome word proceed from your mouth, but only such a word as is good for edification" must be taken seriously by anyone who wants to build a family God's way (Eph. 4:29). Merely talking to one another isn't enough. What is needed is good talk, which blesses rather than blasts, helps instead of hurts, and builds up instead of tearing down.

Good Speech Is Truthful

Good talk has truthful content. Paul says, "Each of you must . . . speak truthfully to his neighbor, for we are all members of one body" (Eph. 4:25, NIV). Truthfulness with others begins with being truthful to yourself about yourself. Scripture warns us often of self-deception. James writes of the danger of being self-deluded (James 1:22). Jeremiah informs us that our hearts are more deceitful than all else (Jer. 17:9). The writer of Proverbs asserts that we are often so self-deceived that we aren't aware of how sinful we are (Prov. 16:2). In many of his epistles Paul sounds the same note. To the Corinthians he writes, "Let no man deceive himself" (1 Cor. 3:18). He urges the Romans not to think more highly of themselves than they ought to think (Rom. 12:3).

The Truth Sometimes Hurts

Being honest about ourselves isn't always easy. At times, it is humiliating, even painful and frightening, to see ourselves as we really are. In counseling I have seen people deny the truth about themselves in spite of incontrovertible evidence. People who were unquestionably abusive, critical, contentious, and malicious have dogmatically asserted that none of these things was true of them. Some of these people realized their guilt and later acknowledged it. Others seemed genuinely to have convinced themselves of their innocence.

Because of the pain that may come from "truthing it," refusing to acknowledge the truth is often regarded as the safe course. Actually it prevents us from developing the relationships God intended us to have with himself and others. Those relationships can only be built on the foundation of openness and honesty. And we cannot be honest with God or others if we're not willing to speak the truth to ourselves.

Sometimes, as the old saying puts it, "the truth hurts." However, it must also be stated that dishonesty and hiding what we really are from others will do more harm. Eventually, people and relationships are hurt more by deviousness and deceit than by the truth appropriately spoken. Disclosing the truth may be like having a necessary operation. The pain is real, but the result is wholeness rather than death.

Walking in the Light

Several verses in 1 John help us to understand why openness and honesty are crucial to wholesome relationships. "If we say that we have fellowship . . . and yet walk in darkness, we lie and do not practice the truth; but if we walk in the light as He Himself [God] is in the light, we have fellowship with one another, and the blood of Jesus His Son cleanses us from all sin" (1 John 1:6, 7).

Carefully note two important statements about true fellowship in this passage.

1. True fellowship with God or others is impossible for people who walk in darkness. "If we say that we have fellowship . . . and yet walk in darkness, we lie. . . ." And what does it mean to walk in darkness? A. W. Pink has explained it well:

> Is it not simple insincerity, the want of perfect openness and transparent honesty . . . ? Is it not that we have in us and about us something to conceal or to disguise? . . . I am not willing to have all that I do and all that I am brought fairly out and placed fully in the broad clear light of truth. I would wish it to be excused, or explained, or somehow obscured or colored; huddled up or hurried over. I am not for having it exposed in the glaring sunshine.[2]

2. John says, "If we walk in the light . . . we have fellowship. . . ." Walking in the light is a prerequisite for true fellowship with God and others. What does it mean to "walk in the light"? Again, A. W. Pink's comments are helpful: "Light is clear, transparent, translucent, patent and open, always and everywhere. . . . The entrance of light . . . spreads reality all around. Clouds and shadows are unreal; they breed unrealities. Light is the naked truth."[3] Building on this definition, we may deduce that walking in the light means that we must be truthful and open with ourselves and with others. That means we should be appropriately honest about our faults, sins, thoughts, and feelings. It means practicing a lifestyle of being real and transparent.

Hiding or excusing our inner selves, including our sins and weaknesses, prevents us from developing relationships that have depth. "If we say that we have no sin" or "if we say that we have not sinned," we not only "make Him a liar" and deceive ourselves (1 John 1:8,10); we also make true fellowship impossible. We must walk in the light even to the point of being open about our sins (1 John 1:9). Jesus indicates that people who don't want to be exposed stay away from the light, but people who aren't afraid to be plainly seen and known come to the light (John 3:20, 21). They don't pretend to be something they are not.

The Unpretentious Paul

Many of the apostle Paul's letters indicate that he was able to establish deep and abiding relationships with people very quickly. Undoubtedly one reason for this was his practice of "walking in the light." He described the way he related to people in these words: "Our mouth has spoken freely to you, . . . our heart is opened wide"; "by the manifestation of truth commending ourselves to every man's conscience in the sight of God" (2 Cor. 6:11; 4:2).

In his ministry and in his interpersonal relationships, Paul didn't put on airs. He didn't pretend to be something he wasn't. He had nothing to fear from people because he was up front with them about himself, his convictions, and his message. What people saw and heard wasn't a facade or a public-relations attempt to create some kind of image. He spoke freely and openly. He opened wide his heart and allowed them to know the real Paul.

Paul's practice of "walking in the light" shines through many of his writings. To the Corinthians, he transparently acknowledged his personal anguish, fears, and concerns about various issues, risking the possibility that they would use this information against him: "For out of much affliction and anguish of heart I wrote to you with many tears . . ." (2 Cor. 2:4); "But I have sent the brethren, that our boasting about you may not be made empty in this case . . . lest if any Macedonians come with me and find you unprepared, we (not to speak of you) should be put to shame by this confidence" (2 Cor. 9:3, 4); "I am afraid that when I come again my God may humiliate me before you" (2 Cor. 12:21). "I determined this for my own sake, that I would not come to you in sorrow again" (2 Cor. 2:1). "And I was with you in weakness and in fear and in much trembling" (1 Cor. 2:3).

To the Romans, he spoke freely about his personal struggles and failures: "For that which I am doing, I do not understand; for I am not practicing what I would like to do, but I am doing the very thing I hate. . . . I know that nothing good dwells in me, . . . for the wishing is present in me, but the doing of the good is not. For the good that I wish, I do not do; but I practice the very evil that I do not wish" (Rom. 7:15, 18-19). Paul agreed with John that true fellowship with God and with other people requires being open and honest about yourself and what's going on in your life, about your struggles and failures.

Game-Playing in Relationships

We often have trouble following the examples of Jesus, John, and Paul. It's easier to slip into game-playing in our interpersonal relationships. Most of us engaged in this during courtship. Wanting to make a good impression on the person we were dating, we were careful to be on our best behavior. On some issues, we didn't let the other person know what we really were like or what we actually thought, lest he or she be put off by our objectionable ideas or behavior.

Putting one's proverbial "best foot forward" isn't limited to dating and courtship. It's much more pervasive than that. Christians may behave quite differently among other Christians than among nonbelievers. Students or employees may be respectful when the professor or employer is present, but disrespectful when he or she is absent. People may talk cordially to certain individuals face to face, but slander them behind their backs. Married people may show each other courtesy in public, but rudeness and insensitivity when they are alone.

I often hear people say: "My spouse isn't the same person I married. Before we were married, he/she didn't think, feel, or behave as he/she now does. If I had known this was going to happen, I never would have married." When I hear someone talk this way, I am inclined to say two things: (1) "Of course, your spouse has changed, but then, so have you. Everybody is constantly in the process of changing. We have new experiences. We get older. We face new problems. We are either getting better or worse." (2) "Your spouse probably hasn't changed as much as you think. You're probably now getting to know the real person you married. Previously, either he or she kept hidden many of the things that annoy you, or you were focusing on the qualities you liked and didn't even notice the problems."

Game-playing after the wedding becomes more difficult because of the fuller exposure couples have to each other. Even so, they still play "let's pretend" or "hide and seek." After the wedding, people continue to withhold what they consider embarrassing or threatening information about themselves from family members. For various reasons, they refrain from being sufficiently open and honest with each other.

In marriage and family counseling, I sometimes ask people (usually when other family members aren't present): "How open and honest are you willing to be with the rest of your family? Do you share 100 percent, 90 percent, 80 percent, 70 percent of yourself?" If the answer suggests that they are not sufficiently open and honest, I then ask two more questions: (1) "What are your reasons for not being more open and honest? What is it that keeps you from doing this?" (2) "What sort of information are you prone to withhold? What things would you be reticent to share?" I do this because I know good family relationships can't flourish when people withhold necessary information. Some of the reasons for not sharing are divisive and injurious themselves. If someone withholds the truth in order to maintain power, to punish, to make peace at any price, or to protect himself, the dysfunction will increase until he is willing to change his style of relating to other family members.

Communication Levels and Styles

In any growing relationship, people must communicate with one another on several different levels. Deep, harmonious, and intimate family relationships are sustained when people utilize a number of communication styles. Each of these styles is important and should be employed in appropriate proportions by all members of the household.

Much conversation occurs on the level of *clichés*, such as "Good morning," "Nice to see you," "It's a beautiful day, isn't it?" or "Hello, how are you?" Such communication is essential to starting conversations. It's a safe means of testing the waters to see if the other person is open to deeper dialogue. At this first level we run little risk of being ignored or rejected.

Level-2 communication involves *reporting facts or information*. When a husband tells his wife what happened at work that day, and she tells him what she did at home, they are engaging in level-2 speech. On that level a person shares little of himself; he is merely functioning as an objective reporter. Though communicating the facts is essential, relationships will remain superficial if conversation goes no deeper than this.

Imparting ideas, evaluations, or judgments, or inviting another person's analysis of certain facts or events takes us down to a deeper strata of communication. Conversations on the level-3 stratum usually begin with such phrases as: "In my opinion . . . ," "I think that . . . ," "In my judgment . . . ," "What do you think about . . . ," or "Give me your honest evaluation of . . ." Because sharing of this sort requires personal disclosure, it promotes the development of intimate, satisfying relationships.

Some people are hesitant to enter into level-3 communication because they want to protect themselves or others from pain, or because they are intimidated by disagreement of any kind. As long as they keep their opinions to themselves, no one can say: "That's ridiculous! I don't see why in the world you could ever think that way." And as long as they don't ask for someone else's evaluation or ideas, they will not receive advice that they don't want to hear. To these people, it seems much better to keep their opinions and ideas to themselves. That way, they don't run the risk of offending others or being rejected.

Appropriately acknowledging and expressing our real feelings is the fourth and deepest dimension of truthful communication. Nowhere does the Bible tell us to deny our feelings and pretend that they don't exist. In fact, Scripture warns us against hypocrisy in reference to our true feelings (Prov. 26:23-28). Many passages clearly encourage us to acknowledge our emotions and then, if they are God-honoring, to enjoy them. Conversely, if they are not approved by God, we are instructed to recognize them and deal with them. For example, the Bible warns us against sinfully dumping our angry feelings on others: "A fool gives full vent to his anger . . . " (Prov. 29:11, NIV); "In your anger do not sin" (Eph. 4:26, NIV); "A fool's vexation is known at once . . ." (Prov. 12:16). These admonitions can only be fulfilled if we acknowledge and appropriately express our emotions. Note carefully what they suggest we should do with our anger: ". . . a wise man holds it [his anger] back" (Prov. 29:11). We are instructed to control our anger, not deny or repress it. "Be angry" (Eph. 4:26), but "in your anger do not sin" (Eph. 4:26, NIV). ". . . a prudent man conceals dishonor" (Prov. 12:16). We are to confess our anger and express it in a constructive way, not in a dishonorable way.

That means that at times we must acknowledge what we are feeling—both the positive and the negative, the pleasant and the not so pleasant—to ourselves, to God, and to each other. The Bible offers many examples of godly people who did this very thing. Frequently you will find the psalmist honestly confessing to himself, to God, and to others that he is anxious and despondent (Pss. 38, 42) or joyful and exultant (Pss. 16, 145). On many occasions Paul makes his feelings known (1 Cor. 2:3; 2 Cor. 2:1-4; 6:10; 7:4, 6). And Scripture makes numerous references to the emotional life of our Lord Jesus. He expressed a wide range of feelings, including compassion, joy, sorrow, concern, and anger. Not one to deny his thoughts or feelings, he was in this area, as in all others, the Truth (John 14:6).

These healthy, mature individuals were in touch with their emotions and were not ashamed to admit them to God and others. They used them not as weapons to inflict wounds on others, but constructively. And they encourage us to do the same.

When You Don't Know What You Think or Feel

At this point, some people express reservations. "I'm just not a thinker. If you want an intellectual, you should have married someone else." "I can't share my insights because I really don't know what I think about many things." "I don't share my feelings because I'm not an emotional person. And besides, even if I have feelings, I don't know what they are. How can I share them?" "I'm not a feeling-oriented person. I'm just not the mushy, sentimental type. I really don't get excited about anything, nor do I get depressed or anxious. I just take things as they come." "It's just not my personality to be emotional. And I can't become what I'm not."

Statements like these may be evasive or excuse-making tactics for people who keep quiet to protect themselves or control others. One woman whose husband explained himself this way told him: "I don't believe you. Don't tell me you aren't emotional. I have seen how animated you become when you are watching sports on TV! I've heard you express your thoughts as you talked back to the television set. You are in touch with your thoughts and emotions when you want to be. You just don't care enough about me or the family to communicate with us."

This woman's assessment of her husband accurately describes why some people don't talk about their thoughts or emotions. But there are others who sincerely struggle to identify their thoughts and feelings. Sometimes this inability is situational—it happens in certain situations, at certain times, with certain individuals. In other cases the inability is pervasive and continuous. There are people who have never been trained to think or feel properly, or they have been trained to squelch their feelings and thoughts so much that they are out of touch with these aspects of their personality. They simply do not have the categories or the expertise to describe what is going on inside them.

When asked what they think or feel, sometimes the most honest answer they can give is "I don't really know." While it is true that people can become more skillful in this area of their lives, pressuring these folks to come up with an immediate answer will only lead to more frustration. They need time to sort their thoughts out before they talk. Accepting without condemnation their willingness to share (no matter how little) and encouraging them when they do will help them open themselves more freely and perceptively.

How to Build Communication Skills

Those who struggle to identify and express their true inner thoughts and feelings may benefit from the following exercises:

1. Use a Bible concordance and do a study on the feelings and emotions of Jesus and other Bible characters.

2. Observe how godly people identify and express their ideas and feelings.

3. Learn to define different emotions accurately—you can't identify or express what you can't label.

4. Give yourself permission to think and feel—you may do so because God gives you permission.

5. Recognize that denying what you are thinking and feeling is harmful, while appropriately acknowledging, expressing, and dealing with your thoughts and feelings is helpful.

6. Monitor your thoughts and emotions. Deliberately tune in on what is going on inside you; periodically ask yourself, "What am I thinking or feeling now?"

7. Actually talk about your thoughts and emotions with others. Be willing to run risks. Deliberately make an effort.

8. Make improvement in this activity a matter of prayer. God can and does understand. He made you with these capacities and wants you to use them.

9. Enlist the help of others. Request their prayer, patience, suggestions, instruction, and feedback.[4]

One goal in family communication should be to develop relationships to the point that we can be open and honest with each other about anything that is important to our personal growth, our relationships with each other, and our relationship with God. Whatever contributes to this kind of growth must be shared.

A Word of Clarification

Having said all this, I want to make it clear that I'm not proposing that we share absolutely everything we think or feel with family members. You will notice that I have frequently qualified open and honest speech with the words "appropriate," "proper," or "constructive." Earlier chapters have urged the elimination of some kinds of speech from our lives. Chapter 10 will explain other guidelines. The point of this chapter is that we must be open and transparent about anything that is important to our relationships and to our growth in the Lord Jesus Christ, even if it may cause some pain or tension. Certainly when the Bible teaches us that we must not let the sun go down upon our anger (Eph. 4:27), it means that we cannot ignore our feelings and pretend they don't exist. Moreover, this passage teaches us that controversial issues associated with our feelings can't be swept under the rug. Somehow these issues must be resolved. We may need to resolve them between ourselves and God as we seek God's help in covering a multitude of faults (1 Pet. 4:8). Or if overlooking them would be detrimental to the other person, our relationship, ourselves, or other people, we must openly, honestly, and biblically deal with the issues troubling us. Otherwise the Bible says we will be allowing the Devil to wreak havoc in many spheres, including our own lives and relationships (Eph. 4:27).

Truth or Consequences

Making mountains out of molehills, nagging, or nit-picking over inconsequential matters is a grave danger to be avoided (Prov. 17:9). But refusing to be honest with yourself and others about important issues is equally serious and can do great damage to families. I have seen situations in which people have denied, minimized, excused, and justified difficulties for years. Burying their true feelings they would say: "What he/she does really doesn't bother me. It's no big deal." "It's such a little thing." "In general we have a great relationship; it's just that ..." Finally, they would reach their limit and assert that they could not (or would not) take it any longer. Out of frustration, hurt, and despair, they would often do something unbiblical or unconstructive. Not knowing what else to do, they would decide they were not going to take it anymore and either throw out an ultimatum or throw in the towel.

Until then they may have thought that they were withholding the truth to keep peace in the family. Instead their refusal to deal with the issues in an appropriately open and honest way gave the

Devil a foothold in their home. (More about this in chapters 12-14).

Proverbs 26 tells of a person who deceives with his lips by fervently declaring his admiration and appreciation while his internal attitude is quite the opposite (Prov. 26:23-28). Scripture says that this man's words are "like an earthen vessel overlaid with silver dross..." (v. 23), in other words, a clay pot thinly covered with a silver glaze. At first his speech may sound good and convincing, but eventually the thin coat of silver wears off and his real attitudes and feelings surface.

Scripture makes it clear that this man thinks his refusal to acknowledge the truth will avert pain and do the most good. In reality his behavior produces hurtful consequences: (1) He crushes and ruins others (v. 28); (2) he gets caught and trapped (v. 27a); (3) what he has done to others happens to him (v.27b); (4) his lack of honesty is exposed (v. 26b); (5) others lose confidence in him (v. 25); (6) what he has done is an expression of hatred and wickedness (vv. 24, 26, 28).

How would you answer the following questions?

> •"Do I speak the truth to other family members, or am I deceitful— withholding truth that is important for our mutual growth?
> •Am I as open, honest, and transparent as God would have me to be, or am I holding others at arm's length?
> •Do I allow others to really get to know me, or do I present a false picture of who and what I am?"

Telling the truth even in the right way may hurt, but refusing to do so will eventually hurt a lot more. Right now, commit yourself to the kind of openness and honesty that God requires for building your family his way.

Study and Application Assignments

Do the assignments individually, then discuss your answers with your mate or your study group.

1. Reflect on the teaching of this chapter and answer these questions:

   a. Why is being open and honest with God and others sometimes so difficult?

b. What was meant by the statement that disclosing the truth may be like having an operation?

c. What does 1 John say is a prerequisite for true fellowship?

d. In what sense do those who walk in the light have nothing to fear from other people?

e. What does this chapter mean by "game playing"?

f. Can you think of any illustrations of "game playing" from your own life or from your observation of other people?

g. Why is "game-playing" a hindrance to family relationships?

h. What may be happening when someone says, "My spouse isn't the person I married"?

i. Answer these questions: How much of yourself do you share with other family members? What are your reasons for not sharing what you withhold? What types of things do you keep from other family members? Are your reasons for not sharing valid? Would your relationships be better if you were more open?

j. What are the different levels of communication mentioned in this chapter?

k. How much of your conversation consists of level 1?___ Level 2?___ Level 3?___ Level 4?___

l. Why do some people refrain from openly sharing their thoughts and feelings?

m. What guidelines for developing communication skills were given? Can you add any other helpful suggestions?

n. What caution did this chapter propose for being open and honest?

o. How does withholding the truth give the Devil an opportunity to hurt the family?

p. What hurts more than telling the truth? Do you agree? If so, why? If not, why not?

q. Do you know of examples—either biblical or extra-biblical—that illustrate the damage that can be caused by not speaking the truth?

2. Select several of the following passages (or if you desire, study all of them) and note what they say about the importance of truthfulness or openness and honesty. Some passages offer good examples to be followed; others, bad examples to be avoided. Describe the results produced by speaking or withholding the truth; "a" and "b" are examples.

a. Psalm 51: David is open and honest with God and others about his sinfulness. He freely acknowledges that he is sinful, that God is just in attributing guilt to him, that he has not been truthful with God, that he needs to be purified, that he has lost his joy and gladness, that he needs a clean heart, and that he is guilty of murder (he speaks of bloodguiltiness, etc.). He confesses all of this to himself, to God, and to others, as is evidenced by the fact that we are reading it today. Then too, the Psalms were the hymnbook of the Old Testament people of God, so apparently this psalm was sung by others who knew David. He wasn't hiding or pretending. As a result, David was forgiven, cleansed, and given opportunity to instruct and warn others.

b. Genesis 4:1-13: Cain didn't speak the truth about his knowledge of where his brother was. He tried to hide from God, but God wasn't fooled. He charged Cain with the crime and pronounced sentence on him. Cain's evasive tactic simply landed him into more trouble and compounded his guilt.

c. Song of Solomon 1:12-16

d. Song of Solomon 2:14

e. Song of Solomon 4:9-11

f. Song of Solomon 5:4-6, 8

g. Song of Solomon 5:10-16

h. Genesis 12:10-20

i. Genesis 26:1-17

j. Genesis 27:1-44

k. Genesis 37:23-35

l. Exodus 32:1-4, 19-25

m. Matthew 26:69-75

n. Acts 5:1-11

o. 1 Samuel 12:1-5

p. John 1:43-51

q. Psalms 42, 43

r. Psalm 73

s. Psalm 77

t. Romans 7:14-25

u. 1 Thessalonians 3:1-5

    v. Mark 3:1-5

    w. John 11:31-38

    x. Matthew 26:36-41

    y. Luke 7:36-50

    z. Acts 20:19, 32

3. Select four or five of the following verses (or if you desire, study all of them) and note what each has to say about being honest and truthful.

    a. Proverbs 12:19: "Truthful lips endure forever, but a lying tongue lasts only for a moment" (NIV). Over the long haul, being honest will pay off. E.g., the respect and confidence people have in you will continue to build; relationships will be maintained. Being dishonest may seem to pay off temporarily, but sooner or later (probably sooner) you will be found out and suffer for it.

    b. Proverbs 14:25

    c. Proverbs 19:1

    d. Proverbs 23:23

    e. Proverbs 24:23-26

    f. Proverbs 27:5, 6

    g. Proverbs 28:13

    h. Psalm 32:2-5

    i. Psalm 51:6

    j. Psalm 62:8

    k. 1 John 1:7-10

    1. 1 John 3:18

    m. James 5:16

    n. 2 Corinthians 4:1, 2

    o. 2 Corinthians 6:11-13

    p. 1 Thessalonians 2:3-6

4. Discuss with your mate how your family is doing at being open and honest. Your answers will likely reveal ways in which family communication can be improved. Then use the list of questions that follow the rating scale to help you in your evaluation. Rate your family communication level by putting a check mark at the appropriate place on the scale. Spend some time planning and praying about making the desired improvement.

Our family communication is:

Excellent, couldn't be better. ___

Good, but could stand some improvement. ___

Fair, in need of considerable improvement. ___

Poor, needs much improvement. ___

a. Does either of you desire to be more open and honest with the other?

b. With the children?

c. The children with you?

d. Are there members of the family who keep you at a distance? Do you wish you knew some members of your family better?

e. How can you help them to become more willing and able to disclose themselves more fully to you?

Notes

[1] Charles Hodge, *Commentary on the Epistle to the Ephesians* (Grand Rapids, Mich.: Eerdmans, 1954), p. 268.

[2] A. W. Pink, *An Exposition of 1 John* (Grand Rapids, Mich.: Associated Publishers and Authors, 1971), pp. 16, 17.

[3] Ibid., p. 15.

[4] Chapter 6 of this book explores this kind of behavior and how to overcome it. You may want to review that chapter.

10

Now You're Really Talking

Communication worthy of the name "real talk" includes being open and honest with one another, but that is not its only component. Real talk is like a diamond. It has many facets, all of which are essential parts of the whole.

Properly Motivated Speech
Several words in Ephesians 4:29 emphasize that "real talk" occurs when people have *proper motives* for speaking. We must be concerned not only about what we say but also about why we say it.

Paul instructs us to speak "only such a word as is good for edification" (NASB) or "only what is helpful for building others up" (NIV). According to this verse, every word—not just some or even most—must be for the purpose of edification. The Greek word for "edification" was used to describe the work of a carpenter or mason—one motivated by a desire to build, not to tear down.

In 1987 we made a contract with a Christian man to build us a house. We worked with him in planning all the details. Then we watched as he and his men dug the basement, laid the foundation, put up the external walls and did all the other things that needed to be done. Fortunately for us, they didn't use inferior materials or do sloppy work. They were careful to do only what "edified" our house. And when they were finished, we literally had no complaints—we still don't. We can honestly say that if we were to build another house, we would be glad to employ the same contractor. He has proved himself to be a good "edifier" of houses.

Similarly, we are called by God to be edifiers of people, especially other family members. As builders of people, we must be just as careful—in fact, even more so—about the quality of our materials and workmanship. Paraphrasing Paul, I believe he is saying: "Be assured that nothing you put into this edification project is more significant than the words you use. Every word you speak will either build someone up or tear him down. Make sure that whatever you say is motivated by a desire to build others up. If it isn't, don't say it."

To underscore the importance of properly motivated speech, Paul uses a second phrase that virtually repeats the statement we have just examined. At the end of the verse, he tells us to make sure that our talk is intended to "benefit [or "give grace to"—NASB] those who listen" (Eph. 4:29, NIV). Demonstrating our intelligence or cleverness must not be the purpose of our speech. Neither should we speak to vent our frustration, to get even, or to put someone else down. In our conversation we are called by God to "do nothing from selfishness [out of competitiveness or self-seeking] or empty conceit [out of a desire for self-exaltation or self-promotion]." Rather, "with humility of mind," we are to regard others as more important than ourselves, not merely looking out for our own interests, but also for the interests of others (Phil. 2:3, 4).

Think of the dramatic impact these directives would have for our families if each person would conscientiously apply them to his communication efforts. Imagine what our families would be like if all competitive, self-promoting talk were eliminated!

To say that we should speak only such words as will minister grace to others doesn't mean that we should never share negative things or negative feelings with other people. Nor does it imply that we should never offer constructive criticism. What it does indicate is that when we speak, we must be honestly convinced that what we say—whether negative or positive—is beneficial to the other person. All negative talk must have a positive purpose.

Fulfilling Paul's directive about properly motivated speech doesn't mean that our conversation must always focus on extremely heavy issues or be filled with quotes from the Bible. Even chit-chat may benefit in building up others. It can break down barriers, establish contact, and lift people's spirits. It can also make people feel comfortable and ready to talk about more substantial issues.

Structuring our conversation along the lines suggested by Paul in Philippians 4:8 would be an excellent way of building up others. If, as Paul instructs, we think and talk about whatever is true, noble, right, pure, lovely, admirable, excellent, and praise-worthy, we will speak words that minister grace to those who listen.

All too often, family conversation tends to be of a "downbeat" sort, filled with complaints, rebukes, criticisms, unpleasant news, disappointments, failures, and difficulties. Certainly, being open and honest with one another requires some interaction of this sort. Nevertheless, two cautions are in order concerning negative con-versation. First, we must be certain that it will serve a positive purpose. And second, we must endeavor to make most of our talking positive rather than negative.

The Greek word translated "give grace" or "benefit" can mean to give favor or help to others. Understood in this way, "real talk" occurs when we give sincere expressions of appreciation to other family members. Providing positive biblical insight, encouragement, comfort, instruction, and correction would also be examples of this kind of good speech.

In keeping with this biblical emphasis on the positive (Phil. 4:8; Eph. 4:29), communication researchers interestingly assert that unless our positive speech outweighs our negative speech by a seven-to-one ratio, people will tend to be put off by us. Your own experience will confirm this observation. Whom have you found most helpful to you? Whom are you most willing to listen to and receive help from? Is it the person whose conversation is primarily negative, or the one whose speech is realistically positive? Is it the person whose words reflect selfishness, or someone genuinely interested in your welfare? The encourager-edifier is the one most likely to benefit you. Regardless of whether the other person speaks the truth, you are not drawn to him or uplifted by his predominantly negative conversation.

Properly Mannered Speech

Speaking to one another in a *proper manner* is another signifi-cant facet in the diamond of communication. Words packaged with bitterness, wrath, sinful anger, clamor, slander, and malice will short-circuit effective communication (Eph. 4:31). But kind, pleas-ant, gracious, and gentle words will facilitate "real talk" (Eph. 4:32). "The wise in heart will be called discerning, and sweetness of speech increases persuasiveness" (Prov. 16:21). "Pleasant words are a honeycomb, sweet to the soul [easy to receive] and healing to the bones [they will be restorative, strengthening, positive]" (Prov. 16:24). "Let your conversation be always full of grace [gracious], seasoned with salt [appealing], so that you may know how [not just what] to answer everyone" (Col. 4:6, NIV).

Suppose I were upstairs in my home and called out to one of my children, "Would you please come upstairs?" On paper that may seem like a simple request meaning only one thing. In real life it could mean several things depending on a number of factors. Among them are the rate of my speech and the tone, inflection, intensity, and volume of my voice. If I speak those words in an angry, demanding tone, they mean one thing. A pleading manner of speech would impart a different idea. A cheerful and gracious tone would convey yet another message.

On occasion, when I have said something to a family member and gotten a less than desirable response, I have either thought or said: "I don't understand why you're so upset. All I said was . . ." Sometimes the disturbing response was prompted by the other person's bad mood or unpleasant circumstances. Often, however, the irritable response reflected the unbiblical manner in which I spoke.

Most of us are very aware that the way others speak to us has a major impact on our response. Unfortunately what we readily acknowledge about the speech of others we tend to forget for ourselves—that the way we speak influences how others respond to us. Speaking in a harsh or insulting manner tends to reap a similar response (Prov. 15:1; 18:6, 7). Conversely, when we use "sweetness of speech," "soft answer[s]", and "pleasant words," we plant seeds that often bear equally desirable fruit (Prov. 15:1; 16:21, 23-24).

Properly Timed Speech

Good communicators constantly ask themselves, "Is this the right time to say what I'm thinking?" Timeliness may make all the difference. Wholesome speech is "according to the need of the moment" (Eph. 4:29). "A man has joy in an apt answer, and how delightful is a timely word!" (Prov. 15:23).

One of the most interesting insights about the importance of properly timed speech is found in Proverbs 27:14: "He who blesses his friend with a loud voice early in the morning, it will be reckoned a curse to him." Blessing other people might include expressions of appreciation or praise, or sharing Scripture or other positive information. Doing it with a "loud voice" indicates enthusiasm and excitement. Instinctively we might assume that such a practice would always benefit a relationship. But God says in effect, "No, there are times when you will get yourself in trouble with other people for enthusiastically blessing them."

How might you upset someone by praising him? The answer: by doing so early in the morning. You may be wide awake, but the other person may still be asleep and not want to be awakened. You may be a fast starter; the other person may not get his motor running properly until mid-morning, and frankly, your enthusiasm tends to irritate rather than encourage him. You can insist that the other person should be like you and continue to relate to him as if he were. Or you can adjust the way you communicate with him at different times during the day, in keeping with the way he actually functions.

There is a time when certain things ought to be spoken, and there is a time when the same things would be better left unsaid. It's possible for my speech to be proper in content, motive, and manner, and yet not be good speech because the timing is wrong. I have learned that there are certain times when my wife appreciates certain suggestions or comments, and other times when she is less than enthusiastic about them. To tell her about a spot on her blouse when she is at home and can do something about it is welcomed. To call her attention to the same spot when she can do nothing about it is not.

A sadder example involved a friend of mine who was physically attacked and abused by someone at a time when she would usually have been in church. Because of this event, she experienced nightmares and had a ferocious struggle with fear and anger. Thoughts about being unsafe and vulnerable dominated her thinking whenever she left home. Was the same attacker lurking in the shadows? Would he be waiting for her in her car? Would he follow her and force her off the road to violate her person again?

In an attempt to overcome her struggles, she shared her situation with one of her pastors. She was looking for some encouragement and godly direction on how to handle her fears and anger. Instead, the pastor, who knew that the attack had taken place at a time when she was usually in prayer meeting, reminded her that if she had been where she should have been, this would have never happened.

Talk about poorly timed, unwholesome communication! What the pastor said may have been true, but his words were certainly not "according to the need of the moment." This young lady didn't need condemnation or rebuke. She needed encouragement, support, and comfort.

I learned a lot about the importance of properly timed speech from an experience I had with one of my sons years ago. I had a speaking engagement close to New York City and decided to take Nathan, who had just gotten his driver's license, with me for fellowship. I asked him if he wanted to drive and, of course, he said yes. We left Philadelphia and headed northeast on the New Jersey Turnpike. As we drew near to New York City, the traffic was horrendous. Cars were zipping in and out of their lanes. One mistake could result in a serious accident. Just ahead of us, our lane and the lane occupied by a large truck merged into one. Seconds later I looked over my right shoulder and caught a glimpse of a tractor trailer vying for our lane. The truck driver sounded his air horn to let us know that the space belonged to him alone. Startled by the horn, my son panicked and put his foot on the brake. "Nathan, don't do that!" I said at once. Immediately he took his foot off the brake and accelerated out of the path of the truck.

Infuriated, the truck driver pulled up alongside of us, rolled down his window, and began to yell at us. After what seemed a very long time, he began to pass by. I warned my son, "Be careful, because he may cut you off and pull over into our lane." And, that's exactly what he did. As his truck got about halfway past us, he began to move over into our lane. We either had to move or be crushed. Happily for us, the next lane was unoccupied, and we eased our vehicle into it.

Now that we were out of danger, I decided I should "strike while the iron was hot" and give my son some much needed instruction on how to drive in traffic. "Nathan," I said, "whenever you are driving in traffic like this, you should . . ." But as I talked, I could tell by the look on his face that he wasn't ready for my counsel. What I wanted to say to my son was true, it was properly motivated, and I think I was prepared to speak in the right manner. But if I had continued my little lesson, it would have been violating the principle laid down in Proverbs 25:20: "Like one who takes away a garment on a cold day . . . is one who sings songs to a heavy heart" (NIV). My son's heart was heavy. He had just had a terrifying experience. He was embarrassed. He wanted to show Dad that he was a capable driver who could be trusted with the family car, and then this had happened.

Seeing his initial reaction, and putting myself in his place, I realized that it was not the time for correction. I dropped the issue, put it in the hands of God, and waited for a more opportune time. That more opportune time came later that evening as we were headed home. My son, who was still driving, turned to me and said: "Okay, Dad, what did I do wrong? What should I have done differently?" The "moment" for speaking had come. Now, I could talk about it to his profit and without hindering our relationship.

The biblical teaching that we call the "golden rule" (Matt. 7:12) certainly has application to communication. At the very least, our Lord's directive about doing for others what you want them to do for you teaches us that you should put yourself in the place of your listeners. Before you open your mouth, think of how you would feel or be tempted to react to what you are about to say. Ask yourself: How helpful is it to me when someone points out my errors immediately after I've had a frightening experience? How do I feel when someone tries to discuss heavy or controversial issues at a time when I'm emotionally and physically exhausted? What happens in me when someone tries to reason with me or correct me when I'm at the peak of anger or frustration? How do I respond to someone who makes jokes when I'm dead serious about something? How do I react when I have done my very best and someone immediately begins to call attention to my mistakes and deficiencies?

Obeying the "golden rule" goes even further than that. Putting it into practice would also involve trying to understand how the *other* person will experience the words you're about to speak. It's not enough to contemplate how you might respond—that's a beginning, but only a beginning. If your words bother the other person and it wouldn't violate Scripture for you to keep silent, then "mum's the word"—keep it to yourself. The time isn't right. To effectively communicate, you must try to understand the make-up and life context of the other person and adapt your speech to suit his or her individuality. That's what you would want others to do for you, and that's what you should do for them.

Timely words are delightful and constructive (Prov. 15:2, 23); untimely words, destructive and damaging (Prov. 18:21). Building your family God's way requires asking, "Is this the right (best) time to say what I wish to say?" That will be a familiar question to people who practice "real talk."

Properly Placed Speech

"Like apples of gold in settings of silver is a word spoken in right circumstances" (Prov. 25:11). God wants us to see that we should be just as concerned (if not more so) about the setting in which our words are spoken as we are about where our finest possessions are placed. When our speech is placed in its proper setting, its benefit is multiplied. The opposite is also unfortunately true. I've heard family members say things about (or to) other family members in public that should have been said in private, if at all. I've ached with husbands, wives, parents, and children as their faults have been unnecessarily and unbiblically broadcast in the presence of others.

Examples of this kind of behavior abound. You'll often hear a husband who doesn't have the courage to talk to his wife about an issue privately taking a pot shot at her in public. You'll hear parents reprimand their children for behavior that could be dealt with much more constructively away from other people.

Some of the insights I've gained about properly placed speech have come through my own communication failures. On occasion I've said things about my wife in front of the children that were not helpful to them or her. In my selfishness I may have wanted her to do something and foolishly made a statement that would have been much more acceptable to her if I had said it in private. Unfortunately, I can also painfully remember times when I have spoken publicly and negatively about the behavior of one of my children. Too often I have had to go to God and to my family asking for forgiveness for my improperly placed speech.

Some of my education in this aspect of "real talk" has also come on the receiving end of wrongly placed speech. Things were said in a group that were probably harmful for others to hear. Things were said to me in public that I would more easily have received were they spoken in private.

If, as Scripture says, "The tongue of the wise makes knowledge acceptable" (Prov. 15:2), then it follows that if it is easier for someone to accept certain information when you're alone with him, that's where the information ought to be shared. You may come to a point where, as Matthew 18:15-17 indicates, you may have to disclose the information publicly in order to help the individual. But as a general rule, negative communication should first be shared privately.

"The heart of the righteous ponders how to answer" (Prov. 15:28). People who want their words to be "like apples of gold in settings of silver" will deliberate over the what (content), the why (motivation), the how (manner), and the when (timing) of their speech. They will also focus on the where (placement) of their communication because they understand the importance of the setting in which things are said.

Words are powerful. They make an impact. Back in 1951 my whole life was changed by hearing some words. I didn't know or care about God. But a friend invited me to a church service, and for the first time in my life, I heard the gospel message. By the end of that night, I was convicted of my sin, as I heard about Jesus and what he had done for sinners. As I listened to the speaker's words, my heart began to long for a relationship with God. So when the opportunity came, I responded to the call of the gospel and received Jesus Christ as my Lord and Savior. Since then my life has never been the same. I became a new creature in Christ Jesus with a new purpose, new desires, and a new destination in life.

What did God use to bring me to the point of commitment? He used words! As I heard them, God powerfully worked in me to irrevocably change my life. "Faith comes from hearing, and hearing by the word of God" (Rom. 10:17). If you're a Christian, this has been your experience also. You heard words about Jesus Christ, about God, about the gospel, and your whole life was changed. That's how powerful words can be! So never underestimate the importance of your words in your family relationships. Though the power of your words cannot be equated with the power of God's Word, your words can and will have a major impact on other family members. Your words matter to God and to others.

God's plan for strengthening your family his way includes the practice of the "real talk" described in this chapter. You can cultivate "real talk" by reflecting on five important questions as a guide to your communication:

1. Am I being appropriately and sufficiently open and honest?

2. Do I have the proper motive for saying what I'm about to say? Will what I'm about to speak be beneficial?

3. Am I ready to say it in the best possible manner?

4. When is the best time? Is this the best time? Is what I'm about to say adapted to the needs of the other person(s)?

5. Where should I say it? Is this the best place?

These five questions highlight important God-given principles for our speech. Make these principles your guidelines for verbal interactions with others. Ask God to help you to implement them more fully in your family relationships. Use these questions and principles as tools for self-evaluation until they are automatically reflected in your speech.

Study and Application Assignments

Complete the assignments individually, then discuss them with your mate or your study group.

1. Reflect on the teaching of this chapter and answer the following questions:

    a. What is meant by the statement that "real talk" is like a diamond?

    b. What words in Ephesians 4:29 emphasize the importance of properly motivated speech? What should be the motivation for our speech?

    c. How can Philippians 2:3, 4 be applied to our communication efforts?

    d. What is meant by the statement that all negative talk must have a positive purpose?

    e. How can chit-chat be beneficial in building up family members?

    f. How does Philippians 4:8 apply to family communication?

    g. What is the 7-to-1 ratio in reference to family communication?

    h. What does this chapter say about the "reaping and sowing" principle of communication?

    i. What communication principle is illustrated by Proverbs 27:14?

    j. What communication principle is illustrated by Proverbs 25:20?

    k. Discuss the relationship of the "golden rule" to family communication.

    l. What communication principle is illustrated by Proverbs 25:11?

    m. What are the five questions that can help us develop the practice of "really talking"?

    n. What other characteristics of good speech would you add to the five that are discussed in chapters 9 and 10?

2. Note what the following verses have to say about characteristics of good speech or "real talk." Identify the characteristic mentioned in each passage according to the categories delineated in this chapter (or make a new category if you need to!).

    a. Ephesians 4:15

    b. Ephesians 4:32

    c. Psalm 141:3

d. Isaiah 50:4

e. Ecclesiastes 12:10

f. Proverbs 12:25

g. Proverbs 15:30

h. Proverbs 16:21

i. Proverbs 22:11

j. Proverbs 25:15

k. Proverbs 31:26

l. Proverbs 31:28

3. Study the following Bible passages and note ways that the people in these passages either did or did not practice "real talk."

a. Ruth 2:1-3:18

b. 1 Samuel 20:27-34

c. 1 Samuel 24:8-15

d. 1 Samuel 25:2-35

e. Daniel 1:8-16

f. John 11:17-44

g. John 21:1-23

4. Take the following "real talk" inventory. Evaluate yourself and other family members on each of the items mentioned. Use the rating scale: almost always do this (= 4), much of the time do this (= 3), sometimes do this (= 2), seldom do this (= 1), never do this (= 0).

My (or another's) speech is characterized by:

a. Honesty.	4 3 2 1 0
b. Accuracy.	4 3 2 1 0
c. Openness.	4 3 2 1 0
d. Motivation to build up.	4 3 2 1 0
e. Grace and graciousness.	4 3 2 1 0
f. A respectful tone.	4 3 2 1 0
g. Encouragement.	4 3 2 1 0
h. A positive tone and nature.	4 3 2 1 0
i. Gentleness.	4 3 2 1 0
j. Warmth and tenderness.	4 3 2 1 0
k. A pleasant tone.	4 3 2 1 0

l. Proper timing. 43210
m. Sensitivity to others' needs. 43210
n. Kindness. 43210
o. Hopefulness and comfort. 43210
p. A servant spirit. 43210
q. Sensitivity to others' interests. 43210
r. Sensitivity to others' moods. 43210
s. Proper placement or setting. 43210

5. Make a list of "real talk" characteristics on which you scored yourself or other family members 0, 1, or 2. Pray about and plan how you can improve these.

11

Getting Your Ears On

A few years back, our family had CB radios installed in our cars. We were doing a lot of long-distance driving and thought CBs would be useful in case we had a breakdown and needed to call for help. They also proved a source of entertainment as we listened in on other CB operators' conversations. We would turn our radios on and frequently hear something like: "This is Big Daddy calling anyone out there. Anybody have his ears on?" Sometimes another CB-er would respond and a conversation would begin. At other times there would be no response; either no one "had his ears on," or everyone was like us and didn't know how to speak the specialized CB language.

In the world of CBs, communication is a two-way street requiring both sending and receiving messages. It is no different in family communication. The listener is just as important as the speaker.

The importance of being a good listener can hardly be overestimated. God himself is our example. Scripture says of God the Father: "For the eyes of the Lord are upon the righteous, and His ears attend to their prayer . . ."; "Then those who feared the Lord spoke to one another, and the Lord gave attention and heard it . . ."; "Behold, the Lord's hand is not so short that it cannot save; neither is His ear so dull that it cannot hear" (1 Pet. 3:12; Mal. 3:16; Isa. 59:1).

Good listening is also attributed to our Lord Jesus Christ. He hears everything God the Father says to him: "All things that I have heard from My Father I have made known to you" (John 15:15). What is more, wherever you turn in the Gospels, you find that when people talked, Jesus was always attentive—whether they were old or young, rich or poor, educated or ignorant, male or female. In CB language, Jesus always "had his ears on."

Scripture portrays the Holy Spirit in the same way. Jesus told his disciples: "He will teach you all things, and bring to your remembrance all that I said to you"; "But when He, the Spirit of truth, comes, He will guide you into all truth; for He will not speak on His own initiative, but whatever He hears, He will speak . . ." (John 14:26; 16:13). Note how Jesus highlighted the extraordinary listening ability of the Holy Spirit. The Holy Spirit heard every word that Jesus said to the disciples, and "whatever he hears, he will speak. . . ."

The fact that our triune God is a good listener should powerfully motivate us to improve in this area. The three persons of the Trinity listen carefully to each other and, amazingly, to us! Have you ever thought of how astonishing it is that God listens to us? This truth should absolutely astound us because of who God is and who we are. That God listens to what we say is also amazing because he already knows what we're going to say before we say it. "Even before there is a word on my tongue, behold, O Lord, Thou dost know it all" (Ps. 139:4). God doesn't need to listen to us to get information or to understand us. He already knows everything perfectly. Yet he patiently listens. What a challenge and example for us!

Paul exhorts us to be imitators of God (Eph. 5:1). If listening is important to God, it should be important to us as his children.

Listening with the Whole Person

What is involved in being a good listener? Proverbs 2:2 encourages us to use our ears and hearts when listening. The ear represents the outer man and the heart represents the inner man. To listen well, according to God, means making your whole self attentive to what is being said.

Listening with Your Outer Man

In several places in Proverbs, God instructs us to incline our ears and hear (Prov. 5:1; 22:17). It's as if God were saying, "When you're listening, lean forward, put your hand behind your ears and bend them toward the speaker." To insist that God means we must literally cup our ears is perhaps pressing the point too far. But certainly we are to give people our full attention.

The acronym "SOLER" can help you remember the physical aspects of good listening. "S" reminds us of the importance of a "squared stance." When listening, don't turn your side or back to the person who is attempting to communicate with you. By facing the speaker you are indicating, "What you are saying is really important to me."

The letter "O" stands for "open stance." A closed stance communicates: "I'm not going to let you close to me. I want to keep you at a distance." In an open stance, the listener relaxes his arms, hands, and shoulders as if to say: "I am here to receive whatever you want to communicate. You have access to me."

"L" in our acrostic reminds us that a good listener "leans slightly forward" when someone else is talking. By doing this he communicates, "I really want to make sure I hear everything you have to say."

The letter "E" stands for "eye contact." A good listener looks right at the other person and avoids giving the impression that he is in a hurry or that his thoughts are elsewhere.

"R" calls our attention to a "relaxed posture." This tells the speaker that the listener is not nervous, ill at ease, or impatient, and sets the speaker himself more at ease.[1]

Listening with the Inner Man

Being "all there" in a physical sense is a fundamental requirement for good listening. But being "all there" in an emotional, mental, and psychological sense—with the inner man—is also necessary.

Listening with the mind. As we shall note more fully later, the Bible makes a clear distinction between "hearing" and "hearing." According to Scripture, you may hear with your ears but not really hear at all. This occurs when you listen merely with the outer man, not with the inner man. Accurate knowledge and an understanding of people require listening with the mind as well as the body (Prov. 18:15).

Listening with the emotions. A good listener practices the admonition of Romans 12:15. He is so focused on the other person that he is able to rejoice with those who rejoice and weep with those who weep. He strives to feel or at least understand what the other person is feeling. We have no good basis for responding to what another person is saying until, to some extent, we have begun to feel what they are feeling. When we respond to people without investing the time and effort to empathize, our relationships and communication will be hollow. People will conclude that we neither understand nor care.

I have often marvelled at the powerful impact the apostle Paul had on people. The New Testament is replete with examples of people whose lives were radically changed through their relationship with him. As I have read of how Paul influenced others, I have wondered what made him so successful. Ultimately, I know that God, the Holy Spirit, chose to use him in an unusual way. Paul could plant and water, but God had to give the increase (1 Cor. 3:6). From another perspective, though, I'm sure that people were drawn to Paul and his ministry because he was a man who related to them with his whole person, with his outer and inner man.

Luke's account of Paul's ministry at Ephesus is one of many biblical passages that portray him as someone who identified with people on the deepest level. During his lengthy stay there, he was with God's people all the time, living where they lived, experiencing what they experienced, suffering with and for them (Acts 20:18, 19). He served the Lord and them with all humility and with great compassion. He listened so well to their verbal and nonverbal communication that he was frequently moved to tears by their burdens and problems. No one could accuse him of being distant, uncaring, trite, or insensitive. No one could say, "But Paul, you don't understand" (Acts 20:18, 31).

Paul's model was Jesus. Three days after the death of Lazarus, Jesus made the journey to Bethany where Lazarus had lived (John 11:1-44). As he approached the town, Mary, Lazarus's sister, came to where he was and fell down at his feet. Sobbing uncontrollably she cried out in anguish, "Lord, if you had been here, my brother would not have died" (v. 32). At this point Jesus already knew that he was going to raise Lazarus from the dead. He could have said: "Mary, get up off the ground. Stop weeping. Don't grieve over what has happened because I'm going to raise your brother from the dead." Instead Jesus carefully listened to Mary with his whole person—his body, intellect, and emotions—and he wept (John 11:35). Only then, having taken the time to identify with Mary, did he go on to raise Lazarus from the dead.

In his attempt to help Mary, Jesus didn't ignore or invalidate what she felt. Because he was going to raise Lazarus from the dead, he knew that there was no real need for Mary's tears, yet he let her cry and even wept with her. What an example of really listening to another person.

Families often violate this principle of good listening. As we listen to another family member, our intellect may tell us that he has no valid cause for what he is thinking or feeling. When a child expresses irrational fears, parents often jump in quickly and explain why his fears are unfounded. When a wife is anxious or upset about a situation, many a husband hurriedly responds with what he considers incontrovertible evidence for the foolishness of such concerns. When a family member gets excited about an opportunity or activity in which you see no value, how easy it is to prick that person's balloon of enthusiasm.

Certainly there is a time for using logic, a time for giving explanations and corrections, a time for showing why certain feelings and responses are unfounded. In general, though, we will be much better prepared to offer words of wisdom and the other person will be much more likely to receive them if we have taken the time to listen with our inner as well as outer man.

Good Listening Requires Discipline and Self-Control

Good listening doesn't come naturally. In numerous places, the Bible commands it: "Make your ear attentive" (Prov. 2:2); "Incline your ear and hear" (Prov. 22:17); "Listen to counsel" (Prov. 19:20);

"Let everyone be quick to hear, slow to speak and slow to anger" (James 1:19). The fact that we are commanded to listen indicates that doing so sometimes requires discipline. At times we may be so weary or preoccupied that we just don't feel like listening. We'll need to exercise self-control, pull in the reins of our minds, and make ourselves pay attention to other people.

I have been in nursing home parlors where the residents have sat facing a television set with the volume turned to the maximum. But if I were to ask what program they were watching, they would not have been able to say because they had allowed their minds to drift. Such inattentiveness is not limited to nursing homes. You've probably allowed your mind to drift when another family member has talked to you, perhaps because the subject wasn't of interest to you.

Sometimes we tune out others when they say something with which we vehemently disagree. That is when the temptation not to listen may be very strong. A husband may need self-control to listen when his wife wants to discuss his insensitivity or wastefulness. A wife may need discipline when her husband wants to communicate with her about their sexual relations or her parents. Careful listening in the midst of volatile parent-child conflicts can take great effort.

It's hard to really listen—and easy to do or say something destructive—when you allow your emotions to take over. That is why James's admonition about listening is accompanied by a command to be "slow to anger" (James 1:19). James knew that once you have lost your cool, you have also lost your capacity to hear what the person is saying. Your unrestrained emotions will cloud your ability to receive and rightly interpret spoken words.

When someone corrects, rebukes, or criticizes you, everything in you may cry out for a quick and forceful response: "Well, no wonder I'm late. You never help with the children. You never lift a finger to help with the dishes or clean up the house." "You think I'm inconsiderate? You don't like me being irritable? Maybe I'd be more considerate and less prone to be annoyed if you would . . ." "I know I shouldn't be as moody as I am and I wouldn't be if you . . ."

When you think you're misunderstood, you may feel like cutting the speaker off and saying: "You've got it all wrong. This is the way it really is." You may have a strong desire to attack the person by pointing out his mistakes. At such times, listening with the outer and inner man, being "quick to hear, slow to speak, and slow to anger" (James 1:19) requires discipline and self-control.

Good Listening Involves Humility

During an early counseling session with Sam and Sue's family, it struck me that Sam did 80 percent of the talking. When I would direct questions to other family members, Sam would cut in on them (and me), adding details or finishing their thoughts for them. He dominated the flow of speech throughout the session, even attempting to control the topics we considered.

As the session came to a close I asked them, "Is what happened today representative of your family communication?" Each person agreed. I didn't tell them why I asked that question, but since I had taped the session, I indicated that I wanted them to go home, listen to the tape and evaluate the way they communicated with each other. "Listen to what is said, how it is said, who does most of the talking, and anything of relevance to the way your family communicates. Next week I want you to come back and tell me what you learned."

When they returned for the next session, I asked them what they had learned. Characteristically, Sam was the first to respond. "I noticed that I talked more than anyone else. I also observed that I sometimes interrupted other people or added to what they were saying." Sue followed: "In our family we do a lot of talking, but I seldom get to talk about the things I want to discuss. We usually talk about what interests Sam. I'm a good listener; I'm ready to hear whatever Sam has to say. I just wish that he would pay attention to me when I want to talk to him about matters I consider important. I've given up trying to communicate with him about a lot of things. He either cuts me off and pontificates about what I should do or gives me the impression that I'm wasting his time and taking him away from more important things."

Sam's poor listening habits violated many biblical directives and proved to be a great deterrent to constructive family relationships. He not only evidenced insensitivity, but also expressed a subtle form of selfishness and pride.

It is pride that says: "Make sure you draw attention to yourself. Choose the topics for discussion. What you want to talk about is more relevant than what other family members may want to talk about. Your problems and concerns are more serious than theirs. Take every opportunity to tell people who you know, how much you know, what you have accomplished. Everyone will be interested in a rehearsal of your experiences and achievements."

Humility stands diametrically opposed to this kind of thinking and behavior. According to the Bible, if you are a wise and humble person you will: (1) appreciate and listen to the counsel of others (Prov. 12:15); (2) respectfully hear what others have to say before you give your opinion on issues (Prov. 18:2); (3) refrain from drawing conclusions or giving counsel until you have really listened carefully (Prov. 18:13); (4) recognize that your viewpoint on an issue may be biased because it is based on insufficient data or colored by selfish interests (Prov. 18:17); (5) carefully consider the insights and perspectives of other people (Prov. 26:12, 16); (6) "be swift to hear, slow to speak and slow to be angry" (James 1:19).

Listening is a way of serving other people. It's a way of esteeming others to be better than yourself (Phil. 2:3). It doesn't take any humility to talk, but it takes a lot of humility to really listen. When we talk, we are on center stage, the star of the show. When we listen, we become a part of the supporting cast.

To listen properly, a servant's attitude and posture is necessary. It requires us to put our whole inner and outer man at another person's disposal saying: "Your interests, concerns, problems, successes, or failures are more important than mine. I will listen to whatever you have to say as long as it is biblically proper. I will allow you to express yourself fully. I yield myself to you. Let's focus on what is most important to you rather than on what is most important to me."

A Special Kind of Hearing

While explaining his parable about the four kinds of soil, Jesus gave us an important insight into what constitutes good listening. He spoke of those who hear but do not hear. On the surface, that may sound like double talk, but Jesus leaves no room for doubt about what he means by this phrase. He adds the explanatory words, "nor do they understand" (Matt. 13:13). According to Jesus, real hearing involves understanding what the other person says in the way he or she means it to be understood. Until this happens, Jesus would say, you haven't really heard the other person.

In counseling, when one family member has accused another of saying something hurtful or offensive, I have often heard the accused say: "I didn't say that. You misunderstood me. Here's what I actually said." For weeks—even months and years—a person may have been stewing over something that had never really been said. He simply had misconstrued the other person without realizing it.

Making sure that you have correctly heard another person's words is one thing—an important first step. But two people may use the same words in different ways. It's been said that the five hundred most commonly used words in the English language have twenty-eight thousand different meanings. I don't know if that's true, but I do know that two people may use exactly the same words and understand those words quite differently.

Just think of the varying ways people understand the words "I love you." The word "right" has many definitions. What it means to be "faithful" or "gentle" or "kind" or "on time" or "considerate" may vary greatly. One person's "discussion" may be another's "argument." "Frugality," "submission," "respect," and "proper behavior" are a few other words subject to numerous interpretations.

In John 2, Jesus' words about "destroying this temple" were completely misunderstood (John 2:19-21). By "temple" he meant his physical body, but the people thought he was talking about the literal temple in Jerusalem. Three years later, they hurled their interpretation against Jesus as an accusation when he was on trial for his life before the Sanhedrin (Matt. 26:59-61).

Jesus' encounter with Nicodemus gives us another illustration (John 3:1-12). In this instance, Jesus had spiritual rebirth in mind when he challenged Nicodemus with the necessity of being born again, but Nicodemus was on a different wavelength. Thinking in terms of physical rebirth, he could not imagine how a grown man could be "born again." Though he accurately heard Jesus' words, he was thoroughly confused and needed to ask Jesus to explain what he meant.

Early in our marriage my wife and I experienced similar misunderstandings. Because we sometimes used similar words in different senses, I would now and then assume that we were completely agreed on an issue when we were not. I would then proceed to act on our supposed understanding, expecting my wife's full support. Only later would I discover that our agreement was not as complete as I had thought, because I meant one thing and my wife meant something slightly or even greatly different.

Different understandings of words and phrases may be problematic in another way too. Two people may think they disagree on an issue when in fact their views are compatible. Frank uses a word or phrase intending one meaning. Dave interprets it differently or more strongly than Frank intended, and responds negatively. Because Frank is unaware of the misinterpretation, he can't comprehend why Dave is getting upset. Thinking Dave is just being unreasonable, Frank finds himself struggling with frustration and anger.

Seeking to ascertain what other people mean by the words they use is the second step on the pathway to understanding. Steps three and four consist of trying to get an accurate reading on (3) what a person is feeling and (4) what he is trying to accomplish through his words. The same words may mean different things depending on the speaker's emotions and his purpose for speaking.

I have sometimes heard my son call his little daughter "a silly goose." By itself this phrase could seem like a put-down. Yet if you would hear my son use these words, you would know that he is expressing love and adoration to his daughter. The tone and warmth of his voice make it clear how much he delights in her.

Good listeners have learned to ask, "What is the speaker feeling and what is he trying to accomplish through his speech?" Suppose I say, "I'm leaving." Could these words be misunderstood? Definitely. Though the actual words are easy to understand, discerning my intended message requires an accurate reading of my emotional state and the purpose for which I have made the statement. Depending on these factors, these simple words might be conveying a number of different messages.

I might simply be giving information to my family about my whereabouts, in case I'm needed. These words might also be spoken in a motivational, invitational way. I might be implying that I hope my wife and children will want to go with me. Then again, my purpose might be protective, punitive, or vindictive. Maybe I'm really upset with someone and want to get away from him because I'm afraid of what he or I might do. I may want to let someone know that I'm so badly hurt that I can't stand to be around him anymore.

Good listening includes seeking to identify the emotions the speaker is feeling and the purpose of his speech. But here's the catch: since you and I are not omniscient and cannot read hearts as Jesus does (John 2:24, 25), we must not make hasty, presumptuous judgments about another person's intentions.

"A fool does not delight in understanding, but only in revealing his own mind" (Prov. 18:2). "He who gives an answer before he hears, it is folly and shame to him" (Prov. 18:13). "The mind of the prudent acquires knowledge, and the ear of the wise seeks knowledge" (Prov. 18:15). "Listen to counsel . . . that you may be wise" (Prov. 19:20). "Let everyone be quick to hear, slow to speak and slow to anger" (James 1:19). "Love is patient, love is kind, and is not jealous; love . . . is not arrogant, does not act unbecomingly . . . bears all things, believes all things, hopes all things . . ." (1 Cor. 13:4, 5, 7).

People who want to become good listeners must apply the principles of these Scripture verses to their listening habits. Looking to God for his grace, Christians must be willing to exercise discipline and do the hard work of developing biblical patterns of listening, which will enable them both to hear and to understand.

Unfortunately it's rare to find someone who will actually make an effort to overcome his poor habits. Becoming a better listener is relegated to the "nice but not really necessary" category. My study of Scripture and my counseling experience has led me to conclude otherwise. For the Christian who wants to build a strong family for God, studying how to be a good listener is part of the core curriculum in God's school of lifelong learning.

God's clear scriptural instructions about listening cannot be taken lightly. Jesus said, "He who has My commandments and keeps them, he it is who loves Me . . ."; "If anyone loves Me, he will keep My word . . ." (John 14:21, 23). Because careful listening is commanded by Christ, it is a way of expressing our love for him. Christ's love for us and our responsive love for him become the motivation for improving our listening skills.

Study and Application Assignments

Do the assignments individually and then discuss your answers with your mate or your study group.

1. Describe your reaction to the content presented in this chapter.
   a. What were the most important points about listening?
   b. Was there anything that was particularly challenging to you in your relationship to your family or to others? Why?
   c. Was there anything with which you disagreed?
2. What is meant by the phrase "listening with your whole person"?
3. What listening principle was illustrated by the story of Jesus and Mary from John 11?
4. When and why does good listening require self-control?
5. Why is humility required for good listening?
6. What is meant by the statement, "To listen properly, a servant's attitude is necessary"? How can listening be a way of serving other people?
7. How will pride and humility manifest themselves in the way you listen?
8. What did Jesus imply about listening when he spoke of people who hear but don't hear?
9. If, as this chapter indicates, understanding is a vital aspect of good listening, what are the four steps for gaining that understanding?
10. What listening principle did the example of Jesus' use of the word "temple" illustrate?
11. What two kinds of family problems may be caused by assuming that

words or phrases mean the same thing to everyone?

12. What does it mean to listen for the intent or purpose of a person's speech?

13. What caution must be exercised when listening for a person's feelings or intent?

14. Why is a faulty interpretation of another person's feelings or intent so dangerous?

15. Complete the following Listening Inventory. Evaluate the quality of your listening patterns on each of the items mentioned. Use the rating scale: never do this (= 0), seldom do this (= 1), sometimes do this (= 2), often do this (= 3), usually do this (= 4). Be honest about your ratings.

When communicating with another family member, I:

(1) Squarely face the other person.	4 3 2 1 0
(2) Express openness through my hands and arms.	4 3 2 1 0
(3) Express interest through my body posture.	4 3 2 1 0
(4) Look at the person who is speaking.	4 3 2 1 0
(5) Am appropriately relaxed, not tense.	4 3 2 1 0
(6) Listen with my mind.	4 3 2 1 0
(7) Listen with my emotions.	4 3 2 1 0
(8) Pace my responses in accordance with the emotional state of the speaker.	4 3 2 1 0
(9) Discipline myself to listen even when I'm tired.	4 3 2 1 0
(10) Discipline myself to listen even when I am not particularly interested in the topic	4 3 2 1 0
(11) Discipline myself to listen even when I don't agree with what is being said.	4 3 2 1 0
(12) Control my emotions as I listen.	4 3 2 1 0
(13) Discipline myself to listen even when I am being rebuked or corrected.	4 3 2 1 0
(14) Am patient, slow to be angry.	4 3 2 1 0
(15) Control my responses.	4 3 2 1 0
(16) Don't dominate the conversation.	4 3 2 1 0
(17) Allow the other person freedom to talk about his interests and concerns.	4 3 2 1 0
(18) Appreciate and listen to counsel.	4 3 2 1 0
(19) Allow others fully to state their opinions.	4 3 2 1 0
(20) Refrain from drawing conclusions or giving advice until I have carefully listened.	4 3 2 1 0

(21) Recognize that my viewpoint may be biased.   4 3 2 1 0
(22) Welcome and solicit the input of others.   4 3 2 1 0
(23) Am eager to hear.   4 3 2 1 0
(24) Seek to serve others by listening.   4 3 2 1 0
(25) Am aware that I may not always accurately hear
     the words another person uses.   4 3 2 1 0
(26) Recognize that we may use the same words or
     phrases with slightly different meanings.   4 3 2 1 0
(27) Try to understand another person's words in the
     way he uses them.   4 3 2 1 0
(28) Realize that my interpretation of another person's speech
     will be influenced by my own emotional condition.   4 3 2 1 0
(29) Realize that my interpretation of another person's
     speech will be influenced by what I perceive about
     the other person's feelings as he is speaking.   4 3 2 1 0
(30) Recognize that my interpretation of another person's
     feelings may be erroneous.   4 3 2 1 0
(31) Am cautious in attributing an evil intent to another
     person's statements.   4 3 2 1 0
(32) Hear people out and don't jump to conclusions.   4 3 2 1 0
(33) Refrain from dogmatically predicting what the other
     person is going to say.   4 3 2 1 0
(34) Acknowledge that the other person knows what he
     meant much better than I do.   4 3 2 1 0
(35) Refuse to use the time when the other person is
     speaking to prepare my response.   4 3 2 1 0
(36) Am slow to interrupt.   4 3 2 1 0
(37) Can accurately summarize and reflect what has
     been said to me.   4 3 2 1 0
(38) Let the other person complete his story.   4 3 2 1 0

16. Note the items on the Listening Inventory on which you scored your-self 0, 1, or 2. Think, discuss, and pray about these items. Plan ways that you can improve on these matters.

Notes

[1]Adapted from Gerard Egan, *The Skilled Helper: Model Skills and Methods for Effective Helping* (Manterey, Calif.: Brooks/Cole, 1986), pp. 76, 77.

PART THREE

SUSTAINING GOD-HONORING FAMILY RELATIONSHIPS

12

Why Families Fight

Why did Paul write to the Roman Christians, "If it is possible, as far as it depends on you, live at peace with everyone" (Rom. 12:18, NIV)? It was because he knew they were having interpersonal conflicts. Other references in the epistle make the same point. "Let us therefore make every effort to do what leads to peace and to mutual edification" (Rom. 14:19, NIV). "Accept him whose faith is weak, without passing judgment on disputable matters" (Rom. 14:1, NIV). Paul was saying: "Brothers, I know you do have conflicts and differences of opinions. But don't allow your differences to drive you apart."

This theme recurs in Paul's first letter to the Corinthians. After a brief introduction, the first issue Paul addresses is the problem of conflicts and divisions: "I appeal to you, brothers, in the name of our Lord Jesus Christ, that all of you agree with one another so that there be no divisions among you and that you may be perfectly united in mind and thought" (1 Cor. 1:10, NIV). The reason for this appeal is disclosed in the next verse: "My brothers, some from Chloe's household have informed me that there are quarrels among you" (1 Cor. 1:11, NIV). Relationships among church members had become strained. Their witness to the world was being marred. These people desperately needed help in learning how to resolve conflicts.

Other New Testament letters contain similar appeals and indicate the immense relevance of the topic of conflict resolution. To the Galatians, Paul writes: "If you keep on biting and devouring each other, watch out or you will be destroyed by each other"

(Gal. 5:15, NIV). To believers scattered among the nations, James declares: "Peacemakers who sow in peace raise a harvest of righteousness. What causes fights and quarrels among you? Don't they come from your desires that battle within you? You want something but don't get it. You kill and covet, but you cannot have what you want. You quarrel and fight" (James 3:18-4:2, NIV). James's point was not merely academic. You can be sure that conflicts were very common among the people to whom he wrote.

Unfortunately the situation is much the same today. We still see Christians bite and devour one another in the home and in the church as they continuously fight and quarrel. In many families, even Christian ones, discord is a normal state of existence.

What about you and your family? Do you ever battle other family members? Have you ever contended with your employer, your work associates, your neighbors, your fellow church members? I'm sure there is not a person reading this book who hasn't had some conflict with somebody. Some have more than others. But if we are honest, all of us will admit that we have had conflicts with other people, including members of our families.

Disagreements Are Inevitable

Occasionally people say to me: "We differ on almost everything. We just can't seem to agree. Certainly, this proves that our marriage wasn't the will of God." My response is that Adam and Eve were tailor-made by God for each other—a perfect match. Yet they became disenchanted with each other. Adam blamed Eve for his eating the forbidden fruit. Eve blamed the serpent. They even blamed God.

Rebekah and Isaac also were specially brought together by God. God led Abraham's servant to Rebekah as he searched for a wife for Isaac (Gen. 24). Yet the book of Genesis reveals that they too had their disagreements. That didn't mean that God had made a mistake. They just needed to learn how to get along.

Contrary to what many think, the difference between a happy and an unhappy home is not the presence or absence of differing views. The basic difference is that in the one home people face and solve their conflicts, whereas in the other they don't know how to. One counselor explains:

> Let us react then against the stupid idea of chance which leads men to imagine that we might hit upon a pearl for a wife as one might a prize in a lottery. Besides, it could be very difficult being married to a pearl if you did not feel yourself in the same category. What really counts then is the working out together of marital happiness. It is a goal to strive after, not a privilege gained at the outset. . . . So-called emotional incompatibility is a myth invented by jurists short of arguments in order to plead for a divorce. It is likewise a common excuse people use in order to hide their own failing. I simply do not believe it exists. There are no emotional incompatibilities. There are misunderstandings and mistakes, however, which can be corrected where there is a willingness to do so.[1]

Here Paul Tournier realistically and biblically states several truths about marital and family happiness. Family members will have some struggles in understanding each other. That is par for the course. Although family happiness will not come automatically, it can be attained by hard work.

"We've Never Had a Conflict"

Some people take issue with that view, saying, "We have never had conflicts in our marriage or family." Such a claim suggests one of two possibilities.

(1) They do have disagreements, but they are afraid to voice them to each other. I remember one such case vividly. An older couple came for counseling because the wife was experiencing deep depression. She saw no point in living. She often just sat around and cried.

I decided to explore her marriage relationship. When I asked her to tell me something about their marriage, she looked at her husband and responded, "My husband and I have never had a conflict." Her husband nodded in agreement.

"You mean you've been married for forty-five years and you've never had a difference of opinion with your husband? You've seen eye to eye about absolutely everything?"

"Oh, I've had differences with him, but we've never had an argument."

"How do you explain that?"

She glanced sheepishly at her husband again and then said meekly, "We don't have arguments because I keep my opinions to myself. Early in our marriage, when I disagreed with him about something, he said: 'Let's not argue! I don't like to argue.' So I learned that we get along a lot better if I just keep my ideas to myself."

Though this woman asserted that she and her husband had never had a conflict, in reality they never had an *external* conflict. Instead she suppressed her ideas to keep peace in the family. For forty-five years she lived in silent turmoil. Though she had the intelligence to make independent judgments and draw different conclusions, she never felt free to share her thoughts with her husband. Their lack of discord was more myth than fact.

(2) The other possibility when people say that they never have conflicts is more positive. The couple may have disagreements, but resolve them before they become conflicts. A disagreement is a difference of opinion primarily on the cognitive, intellectual plain. A conflict is a difference of opinion that affects us severely on the emotional and relational levels. Some people have learned to prevent conflicts by handling their disagreements biblically. It's not that these people are carbon copies of one another. They have their own opinions and share them. But they respond to disagreements in such a way that they seldom become conflicts.

The Pain of Discord

Biblical data, historical records, and personal experience all indicate that in interpersonal relationships disagreements are inevitable. Your personal happiness is affected by the way you handle the disagreements that arise. Scripture declares that it is "good and pleasant . . . when brothers live together in unity!" (Ps. 133:1, NIV). The reverse is also true. Most people would tell you that there is no distress more severe than that which comes from unresolved family discord.

One friend of mine came through a period of intense pain and uncertainty with flying colors. She maintained emotional stability when she almost lost her life, when her ability to function independently was in question, when family members died, and when certain family members were having serious problems. Deep depression enveloped her, however, when a disagreement arose between her and her husband that they could not seem to resolve. That discord affected her personal happiness more than anything else.

The way you respond to disagreements will affect your performance on the job. Many talented, well-educated people flounder in their careers because of their inability to relate to others. An acquaintance of mine had nineteen different jobs in nineteen years. She'd take a job thinking that at last she would be happy, but soon she and her boss or another employee would see things differently. Before long she would become dissatisfied and begin looking for another job. By the age of forty, she experienced severe depression because she looked at her life and saw that she had accomplished very little. Though she was a woman of great ability, her inability to handle conflicts seriously limited her occupational achievements.

Knowing how to handle conflicts is also a critical issue in Christian service. When I came to know Bob and Mary Smith (pseudonyms), Bob had been in the pastorate for twenty years. During that time he had pastored six churches and Mary had experienced five "nervous breakdowns." They had come to see me because Mary was on the verge of yet another breakdown.

Data gathering revealed that in every instance Mary's breakdowns coincided with serious conflicts that arose in the church. In most cases a group of people in the church was unhappy with something the pastor or his wife or family had done. Mary didn't know how to respond to these difficulties. As she would brood over what was happening, she would become hurt, anxious, intimidated, and frustrated inwardly. Outwardly she would pretend nothing was wrong and simply try to avoid the people who were unreasonable and unappreciative. Gradually, the internal pressure would become so intense that she would go berserk.

Bob's way of responding to conflicts was quite different. Mary was an "internalizer," a "suppressor." Bob was a "confronter." When conflicts arose, he would take his stand and carefully and repeatedly explain why his position was right and why other positions were wrong. Finally, people did one of three things: they capitulated, they became polarized in their opposition to Bob, or they withdrew from the church. Eventually, when too many people responded in the latter two ways, the Smiths would move to another church.

Bob and Mary's personal happiness was being destroyed by their sinful ways of dealing with disagreements. More than that, their effectiveness in Christ's service declined severely. They were both gifted people who could have contributed significantly in building up fellow Christians. Unfortunately their contributions were seriously impaired by the way they dealt with conflicts.

The Blessing of Peace

Scripture declares that "peacemakers who sow in peace raise a harvest of righteousness" (James 3:18, NIV). Do you want to produce a harvest of righteousness in your family? James says that you should not expect this to occur in a home marked by fighting and quarrelling. It will happen in families where peacemakers are continuously sowing in peace. They will reap the harvest of righteousness.

Psalm 133 emphasizes the same thought. It compares unity in the family with the anointing oil that was poured on Aaron when he was set apart for his priestly ministry (Exod. 29:7; 30:25). He was thereby officially consecrated for the Lord's use. The psalmist seems to be saying that when we maintain unity (by preventing and resolving conflicts), we, like Aaron, are especially set apart for the Lord's service. In an atmosphere of peace and unity, God blesses and uses us in a special way.

Another phrase in this psalm expands the concept further. The psalmist compares peace and unity among brothers to "the dew of Hermon . . . falling on Mount Zion" (Ps. 133:3, NIV). Between the rains of early spring and late summer, little precipitation fell in Palestine. If the crops were to grow, they needed additional moisture. Fortunately, unless severe conditions prevailed, many sections of Palestine were blessed with a heavy dew. Nowhere, however, was the dew heavier than around Mount Hermon. As a result, the fields in this area usually bore an abundant harvest.

In similar fashion, the psalmist indicates that God's blessing is abundantly bestowed on people (individuals, families, churches) who cherish unity. Drought conditions may prevail all around such people, and evil forces may oppose the work of God in their lives. But in their relationships in and out of the home, the blessing of God yields a harvest of righteousness.

The Three Phases of Marriage

Someone has said that most American marriages go through three phases. Phase 1 is *ecstasy or enchantment*. This takes place during courtship and the early days of marriage, when romance reigns. Everything is wonderful, and one's mate can do no wrong. Whatever minor flaws or differences exist, the couple believes, will not interfere in their relationship.

Phase 2 is the *reality or conflict* phase where marriage partners are forced to recognize that they don't always see eye to eye. Gradually they begin to realize that they didn't marry themselves. They see that the other person has real faults and that they have some strong differences on certain issues. Slowly (or, in some cases, swiftly) conflicts arise between them.

From this reality or conflict phase, couples move in one of three directions. Some couples decide that they can't handle their differences and move toward *divorce*. Others proceed into an *unhappy status quo* where they just coexist. The third group learns how to handle their disagreements and prevent or resolve their conflicts. As a result, they progress into a *maturing relationship or growth and development*. For them, marital or family disagreements provide the context for progress and on-the-job training in applying biblical principles. They reap a harvest of righteousness because they have learned the important skill of resolving conflicts.

But the question is, How do you become a peacemaker instead of a warmonger? What's involved in preventing and resolving conflicts biblically? Understanding why disagreements are inevitable and why conflicts often develop out of them is one important factor. Having a clear answer to the question, "What is the source of quarrels and conflicts among you?" (James 4:1) is a first step.

Sources of Conflict

Members of the same family may differ in personality, perspective, values, gifts and abilities, interests, likes, dislikes, level of education, intelligence, and training. These disparities frequently provide occasion for the disagreements and misunderstandings that can lead to contention. So *differentness* is a major contributor to family conflicts.

Because of the dissimilar gifts and talents God has given us (Rom. 12:4-6), we may have a deeper interest in certain things than other family members do. It's easy for us to think that everyone should be as devoted to a particular concern as we are. If others are not, we can become pushy and communicate that there is something wrong with them for their lack of excitement.

Contrasting styles of decision making can lead to family quarrels. Some people make decisions very quickly, others slowly. One group sizes up a situation rapidly and reaches a quick conclusion, so as not to procrastinate. The other group analyzes and reanalyzes, waiting and gathering more facts before deciding, so as not to act in haste. While the first group may become impatient with the second, the second group may feel pressured by the first, and tension may give way to contention.

Divergent lifestyles can breed problems in the home as well. One sixty-five-year-old couple had been squabbling for years. It was evident that they were opposites in many ways, but especially in the pace of their lives. At sixty-five she was still living in the fast lane. Hurrying wherever she went, she worked full time as a nurse and had no thoughts of retiring. Her husband wasn't at all like that and never had been. He was slow—very, very slow. When he moved, he did so just barely. It seemed that the only thing he did fast was get tired. He had long since retired from full-time employment.

When his wife would leave in the morning, she would ask him to do certain things around the house, and he would respond with an "uh-huh." On her return, she would often find that many of the things were not done. Each time that happened, she would become more upset. He promised to change, but never did to her satisfaction. Eventually her anger intensified to the point that on several occasions she actually took a butcher knife and chased him around the house!

Punctuality is another area in which people differ. For some, being on time or ahead of time is a high priority. Schedules are to be kept regardless of what happens. For others, promptness is not as crucial. If they arrive around the appointed time or at least before an event is over, that's fine. Flexibility and responsiveness to needs are more significant to them than punctuality.

Even such a matter as how food should be prepared may be a catalyst for family discord. A physician and his wife were experiencing severe family disruption. Though conflicts had developed over many things, one of the hottest had to do with food preparation. Because of his concern about cholesterol, he thought she should cook everything with water. She maintained that cooking with the right kind of oil was satisfactory. Besides, she considered the kitchen to be her realm, and she didn't like him telling her what to do in her domain.

Differences in age, training, priorities, values, or experience may account for many variances in viewpoint between parents and children. When relating to their children, parents must make allowance for this age and experience gap. They must keep in mind the words of Paul, "When I was a child, I used to speak as a child, think as a child, reason as a child; when I became a man, I did away with childish things" (1 Cor. 13: 11). Parents must remember that there is a child's way of viewing things as well as an adult way.

The areas in which family members may differ are almost innumerable. I've illustrated a few above. The following list comprises some of the more common issues on which family members may have differing opinions.

1. Concepts of the marriage and family relationship.
2. Husbands' and wives' roles and responsibilities.
3. Occupational and professional objectives.
4. Boundaries between family members (sharing, privacy, free-

dom, individuality, togetherness, etc.) and with people outside the family.

5. Finances.

6. Preferences in recreation and leisure.

7. Church attendance and involvement, spiritual convictions.

8. Expectations concerning the number of children, spacing of children, relationships with children, reasons for having children, training and discipline of children, whether children take priority over one's spouse.

9. How much to demonstrate affection and in what ways.

10. Social relations, friendships.

11. Sexual issues.

12. What constitutes proper behavior, etiquette, customs.

13. Philosophy of life.

14. Relationships with parents or in-laws.

15. Values and goals.

16. How to make major and even sometimes minor decisions.

17. Household tasks; what constitutes a clean house and who is responsible for it.

18. The amount of time spent together.

19. Family devotions, prayers, Bible study (If? What? How? When? How much?).

20. Housing: buying or renting; maintenance and furnishings.

Even in the best of families there are different perspectives. That is a given. Expect it to happen and don't let it throw you. Recognize that not everything is a matter of right or wrong, bad or good; some things are just different. But be on your guard, because differences that are not handled properly can easily turn a harmonious home into a war zone.

Getting to the Root of Conflicts

But why do differing viewpoints so readily turn into conflicts? Scripture declares that we have conflicts because of our desires that battle within us; because we want something we cannot have (James 4:1-3). In other words, differences often turn into conflicts because we are selfish. We want family members to see things the way we do, to believe what we believe, to act as we want them to act, or to do what we want done. And when they won't cooperate, we become frustrated. Then, because of our selfishness, we may respond in any number of sinful ways. We may try to force family members into compliance by nagging, shouting, or incessant arguing. Perhaps we lash out and punish them verbally or even physically. Or it could be that we use more subtle means to pressure them into conformity or to hurt them for disagreeing with us. We may pout, withdraw, cry, or frown, or be silent, uncooperative, or wasteful. Because our desires are being thwarted, our efforts to control the situation produce conflicts.

Think of your own experience. You may feel you're not getting enough emotional support, respect, approval, affirmation, or affection from other family members. You may be looking for more physical help around the home and feel that others take unfair advantage of you. Or maybe you want something spiritually, such as agreement with your interpretation of Scripture, conformity to your standard of right and wrong, or improvement in some family member's walk with the Lord. How do you react when others don't fulfill your desires? And why do you react in the way you do?

James strips away all the pious pretense and gets to the root of many of our interpersonal conflicts. With great boldness and clarity, he explains that if your wishes lead to conflicts in the home, the real problem is your consuming desire for your own satisfaction. James says in effect: "You fight and quarrel because you're selfish. You have wrong motives. You're not really concerned about the glory of God or the good of others. You're mainly concerned about yourself, your reputation, your own pleasure. To get your own way, you'll even attempt to manipulate God and other family members" (James 4:1-3).

Conflict for Righteousness' Sake

Sometimes discord arises for a radically different reason. Scripture reminds us that people will at times oppose us because we stand for righteousness. "Blessed are those who are persecuted because of righteousness. . . . Blessed are you when people insult you, persecute you and falsely say all kinds of evil against you because of me" (Matt. 5:10, 11, NIV).

Christians can expect opposition in society. But Jesus also warns us of similar discord within the family circle. "A man against his father, a daughter against her mother, a daughter-in-law against her mother-in-law—A man's enemies will be the members of his own household" (Matt. 10:35-36). On occasion family discord will arise because someone (a wife, husband, parent, or child) is standing for righteousness and others are opposed to that righteousness.

Abel's righteousness drew the wrath of his brother Cain (Gen. 4). Likewise, Joseph's brothers hated him (Gen. 37). And so, even in a believer's home there are times when family members will become upset at his or her convictions. Occasionally you may even be the one distressed by some righteous conviction or action of another family member. Unfortunately, this side of heaven we are all capable of opposing God's will and becoming annoyed with those who are seeking to obey him.

My wife, for example, may want to reach out to a needy person after a church service. Carol senses that the person is really hurting, and she desires to bear that person's burden and give encouragement. She sees it as an act of righteousness, and she's right! When she asks me if that would be okay, I outwardly assent, but internally dissent. I'm not thinking about what Jesus wants or what the other person needs. All I'm thinking is that I want to get home. I'm hungry. I've had a busy week. I want to put on my old clothes and relax.

When she finally does come to the car (fifteen minutes later), I communicate to her in one way or another that I am opposed to what she did. What's going on here? Well, we're in conflict because Carol wanted to reach out to someone in Jesus' name, but I was irritated with her for her act of righteousness.

Yes, discord will occasionally arise in a family because one member is concerned about righteousness and other family members, at least temporarily, are not. I'd like to think that every time I've had a conflict with another family member, it's because I've been standing for Christ. But in many cases, the reason we have clashed is that I have responded selfishly to our differences or the other person's righteousness. All too often I have been guilty of what James condemns. I have wanted something and not gotten it. Oh, I could give all the spiritual reasons in the world why my desires were right and thereby justify myself for being annoyed. But the truth is that I was suffering more for selfishness' sake than for righteousness.

And what is true of me is often true of others. Because of the nature of my ministry, I am constantly involved in trying to help people who face conflicts in their homes. Some who come for counseling are truly suffering for righteousness. They need encouragement, support, affirmation, prayer, acceptance, and compassion. In other cases, I find that discord is associated with selfishness, unreasonable expectations, an overbearing attitude, a desire to control, jealousy, excessive ambition, insensitivity, ungodly motives, pleasure seeking, idolatry of self (me-ism), and a feeling-oriented life.

People like this don't need encouragement to continue in such attitudes. They need to be called gently to repentance and confession of sin. They need to be urged to turn to Jesus Christ for forgiveness and for the power to change the orientation of their lives. Sinful attitudes and actions must be put off and biblical (Christ-centered) attitudes and actions must be developed by the power of the indwelling Holy Spirit.

Preventing Family Conflicts

How do you prevent and resolve family conflicts? The first step is to be aware that in any close earthly relationship, disagreements can easily become conflicts. The closer your relationship, the greater the potential for contention and discord. To prevent this from happening in your family, recognize the specific ways in which you are alike and in which you are dissimilar. Don't sweep your disparities under the rug. Get them out in the open and discuss them thoroughly.

Then seek to discern the reason why these differences tend to escalate into conflicts. Be honest before God. Ask yourself: Do these differences and disagreements bother me so much because I am being selfish? Is it because I want my own way and the other person isn't cooperating with my demands? Am I envious? Do I have ungodly motives? Diagnose what's going on in your life and relationships by using the Scripture as your standard. Wherever you find your attitudes, thoughts, emotions, and actions to be unbiblical, take full responsibility for them. Don't blame-shift or rationalize! Instead, acknowledge your sins and look to Jesus for his forgiveness. Fix your eyes on him and trust in him to help you to respond to your differences and disagreements in a more godly, constructive way. By his power, family discord can be turned into family concord.

Study and Application Assignments

Do the assignments individually and then discuss your answers with your mate or your study group.

1. Describe your usual reaction(s) to disagreements or conflicts. Analyze the attitudes behind the reactions.

2. What does Scripture indicate about the ease or difficulty of getting along with other people? Support your answer with Scripture.

3. Do you agree with Paul Tournier's statement about emotional incompatibility? Why or why not? Support your answer biblically.

4. Do you concur that disagreements are inevitable? Why are they inevitable?

5. When people who live together say they never have any disagreements or conflicts, what may be happening?

6. This chapter, mentions several reasons why conflict resolution is important. What are they? Identify supporting Scripture. Add your own insights about why resolving conflicts is important. Illustrate from the Bible, history, literature, or your personal experience the debilitating effects of unresolved conflicts.

7. Identify and describe several disagreements and conflicts you have had with other family members. Using the information from this chapter, analyze the reasons why the disagreements arose and why they became conflicts.

8. Complete the Personality Inventory Chart (see below). Evaluate every member of your immediate family. With which family member do you have the most similarities? The most dissimilarities? With which family member do you find it easiest to get along? Hardest? Note how your similarities and dissimilarities have affected your personal and family relationships.

9. Fill out the Conflict Analysis Form (following the Personality Inventory Chart). Note with which of the family members you are most prone to have disagreements. Why do you think that is? How have these disagreements affected your relationships with these persons? How have your disagreements affected the whole family?

PERSONALITY INVENTORY CHART

On a scale of 0-4 rate yourself and every family member on the following qualities. Four is the highest rating and 0 is the lowest. For example, for number 1, if you are very patient, give yourself a 4. If you are not patient at all, give yourself a 0. If you are somewhere in between, rate yourself from 1 to 3. (C. = child.) Circle any area where you and family members rate more than one point difference. Discuss how differences or similarities affect your family relationships.

QUALITIES	SCORES: You/ Mate/ C. 1/ C. 2/ C. 3/ C. 4
1. Patient	__/ __/ __/ __/ __/ __
2. Accepting	__/ __/ __/ __/ __/ __
3. Stubborn	__/ __/ __/ __/ __/ __
4. Easily annoyed	__/ __/ __/ __/ __/ __
5. Resentful	__/ __/ __/ __/ __/ __
6. Forgiving	__/ __/ __/ __/ __/ __
7. Dominant	__/ __/ __/ __/ __/ __
8. Self-centered	__/ __/ __/ __/ __/ __
9. Gentle	__/ __/ __/ __/ __/ __
10. Pushy	__/ __/ __/ __/ __/ __
11. A good listener	__/ __/ __/ __/ __/ __
12. Reasonable	__/ __/ __/ __/ __/ __
13. Considerate, thoughtful	__/ __/ __/ __/ __/ __

QUALITIES	SCORES: You/ Mate/ C. 1/ C. 2/ C. 3/ C. 4
14. A loner	__/ __/ __/ __/ __/ __
15. Depressive	__/ __/ __/ __/ __/ __
16. Open	__/ __/ __/ __/ __/ __
17. Expressive	__/ __/ __/ __/ __/ __
18. Practical	__/ __/ __/ __/ __/ __
19. Efficient	__/ __/ __/ __/ __/ __
20. Neat, organized	__/ __/ __/ __/ __/ __
21. Extravagant	__/ __/ __/ __/ __/ __
22. Reliable	__/ __/ __/ __/ __/ __
23. Affectionate	__/ __/ __/ __/ __/ __
24. Athletic	__/ __/ __/ __/ __/ __
25. Ambitious	__/ __/ __/ __/ __/ __
26. A pleasant voice	__/ __/ __/ __/ __/ __
27. Musical	__/ __/ __/ __/ __/ __
28. A good dresser	__/ __/ __/ __/ __/ __
29. Forgetful	__/ __/ __/ __/ __/ __
30. Lazy	__/ __/ __/ __/ __/ __
31. Outgoing	__/ __/ __/ __/ __/ __
32. Impulsive	__/ __/ __/ __/ __/ __
33. Artistic	__/ __/ __/ __/ __/ __
34. Calm	__/ __/ __/ __/ __/ __
35. Conventional	__/ __/ __/ __/ __/ __
36. An outdoors person	__/ __/ __/ __/ __/ __
37. A spender	__/ __/ __/ __/ __/ __
38. An initiator	__/ __/ __/ __/ __/ __
39. Secure, confident	__/ __/ __/ __/ __/ __
40. Generous	__/ __/ __/ __/ __/ __
41. Aggressive	__/ __/ __/ __/ __/ __
42. Punctual	__/ __/ __/ __/ __/ __
43. Flexible	__/ __/ __/ __/ __/ __
44. Adventurous	__/ __/ __/ __/ __/ __

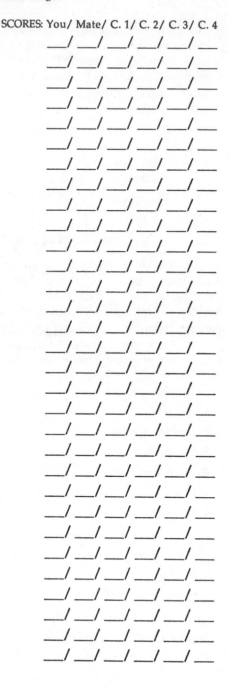

QUALITIES	SCORES: You/ Mate/ C. 1/ C. 2/ C. 3/ C. 4
45. Decisive	__/ __/ __/ __/ __/ __
46. Sentimental	__/ __/ __/ __/ __/ __
47. A procrastinator	__/ __/ __/ __/ __/ __

CONFLICT ANALYSIS FORM

Indicate below the approximate extent of agreement or disagreement between you and other family members for each item in the list. Use this scale (C. = child):

1 = Always agree   2 = Frequently agree
3 = Occasionally disagree   4 = Frequently disagree
5 = Almost always disagree   6 = Always disagree
7 = Not applicable

After you have completed the rating, circle the numbers of the items that pose the greatest potential for conflict.

	YOU: & mate/ & C. 1/ & C. 2/ & C. 3/ & C. 4
1. Use of money	__/ __/ __/ __/ __
2. Recreational matters	__/ __/ __/ __/ __
3. Spiritual matters	__/ __/ __/ __/ __
4. Friends (social life)	__/ __/ __/ __/ __
5. Demonstrations of affection	__/ __/ __/ __/ __
6. Correct or proper behavior	__/ __/ __/ __/ __
7. Philosophy of life; goals	__/ __/ __/ __/ __
8. Time spent together	__/ __/ __/ __/ __
9. Making major decisions	__/ __/ __/ __/ __
10. Leisure time activities	__/ __/ __/ __/ __
11. Career decisions	__/ __/ __/ __/ __
12. Prayer and Bible study together	__/ __/ __/ __/ __
13. Where to live	__/ __/ __/ __/ __
14. What type of housing to live in	__/ __/ __/ __/ __
15. Ways of dealing with grandparents, parents, and in-laws	__/ __/ __/ __/ __

YOU: & mate/ & C. 1/ & C. 2/ & C. 3/ & C. 4

16. Use of alcohol or drugs   __/ __/ __/ __/ __

17. How to resolve disagreements   __/ __/ __/ __/ __

18. Sexual issues   __/ __/ __/ __/ __

19. Family life issues: training and
    discipline, fun times, etc.   __/ __/ __/ __/ __

20. Church attendance and involvement __/ __/ __/ __/ __

21. Marriage and family expectations   __/ __/ __/ __/ __

22. Occupational, scholastic,
    professional matters   __/ __/ __/ __/ __

23. Family chores and responsibilities   __/ __/ __/ __/ __

24. The husband's/wife's roles and
    responsibilities   __/ __/ __/ __/ __

On a scale from 0-10 (0 = lowest; 10 = highest) indicate your overall satisfaction level with your present relationship with each family member.   __/ __/ __/ __/ __

Notes
[1]Paul Tournier, *To Understand Each Other* (Atlanta, Ga.: John Knox Press, 1974), pp. 12, 13.

13

The Peace Officer Every Family Needs

Getting along with other people, even family members, can be painfully difficult. Conflicts and divisions come so easily and yet can be so hard to resolve. But Scripture holds out to us the possibility for people to establish a deep and abiding peace through a unique, specially ordained peace officer with impeccable credentials and unlimited ability. I refer, of course, to Jesus Christ, whom God sent to be our peace, to break down barriers, and to abolish enmity (Eph. 2:13-22). There has never been another peace officer like Jesus. He can do what no other peacemaker can.

To maintain good family relationships, you must prevent and resolve disagreements and conflicts. Jesus Christ specializes in this kind of work. That's why I say that the most critical factor for the prevention or resolution of family conflicts is your own relationship with Jesus Christ. The foundation for conflict resolution is not a technique or a neat little step-by-step formula. Techniques have their place, but they can never automatically produce peace in the family. Your relationship with Jesus Christ is much more important—and practical—than any technique.

Though that's a bold statement, it is easily supported by Scripture and clearly illustrated by personal experience. The apostle John comments on this in 1 John 1:3, 7: "We proclaim to you what we have seen and heard, so that you also may have fellowship with us. And our fellowship is with the Father and with his Son, Jesus Christ. . . . if we walk in the light, as he is in the light, we have fellowship with one another, and the blood of Jesus, his Son, purifies us from all sin" (NIV). Notice carefully what John em-

197

phasizes as the focal point of true fellowship among believers. Our union and fellowship isn't centered in our perfect agreement on various issues, a common educational or racial background, economic status, social concerns, or many of the other things that often draw people together. Rather, John says that Christ is the basis of true fellowship with God and with each other.

As believers, our common union with Christ is the foundation for our union with each other. If we are united to him as the Head, we are united to one another as members of his body. Having peace with God through the cleansing blood of Christ clears the way for harmony with one another. Other things that might divide us pale into insignificance in comparison to our common union and devotion to Christ.

In Philippians 4:2 Paul wrote to two ladies who had a major rift in their relationship. It is likely that Euodia and Syntyche were holding grudges, seething with bitterness, and avoiding one another. The situation had become so serious that their conflict was common knowledge. The church was in danger of being divided into two camps.

On the objective level, these two ladies were united both to God and to each other through Christ (Phil. 4:3), but on the subjective, experiential level the situation was quite different. The news of this problem had reached Paul, hundreds of miles away in Rome. The situation had become so severe that Paul felt compelled to deal with it. How did he attempt to resolve this situation? The answer is simple but profound.

For one thing, he appealed to a mature Christian to get involved and promote unity. He intimated that the emotional climate between Euodia and Syntyche had become so volatile that help from a mature counselor was in order. Next, Paul appealed to both individuals to accept personal responsibility for resolving their differences. In effect, he said: "You both have a problem and I am laying the responsibility on both of you to do something about it. I don't want each of you to wait for the other to straighten out the situation. If you're willing to follow my God-inspired instructions, there is absolutely no reason why your conflicts can't be resolved. You can once again live in harmony."

Paul's help to these ladies came primarily in the form of powerful reminders of certain basic facts. John Gwyn-Thomas describes Paul's approach in this way:

> He did not want them to patch things up superficially, because the animosity would have remained underneath. He wanted to get to the root of the trouble so that they would face up to what was dividing them and be one in the Lord. So he reminds them that the things which united them were far greater than those which divided them, that is, they were both redeemed through Jesus Christ; they both had the same heavenly father and the indwelling Holy Spirit; both of them were going to dwell eternally in the presence of God. He appealed to them to examine themselves in this unifying perspective, involving their minds as well as their heart, so that they would see the triviality of natural differences in the light of this great unity in the Spirit.... he recalls their former unity in the service of Jesus Christ—"they have both labored side by side with me in the Gospel."
>
> The apostle makes one more appeal to these women which is not quite so direct. He wants them to see themselves from a different standpoint. Should they be in conflict with each other when they both have their names written in the book of life? Once again, he is reminding them of a great spiritual truth, which applies to every Christian, namely, that it does not matter how unimportant or insignificant we may appear in the eyes of the world or even the church, our names are in the book of life.... In the end the only thing that will matter is that our names are in that book of life.... As citizens of the heavenly kingdom, we are to be living God's life on earth, we are to act as citizens of that kingdom. Our life is not primarily to be a constant struggle for positions.... If we live this life in the light of eternity, the trivial things are put in the right perspective.[1]

Do you see Paul's focal point for conflict resolution? He doesn't say: "Because things have gotten so bad between the two of you, it's evident your relationship is beyond repair. Your personalities, interests, and convictions make you incompatible. I think it would be best if one of you would remove herself from the church and become involved someplace else." Paul's words indicate that he firmly believed that Euodia and Syntyche could resolve their differences. Nor did Paul try to help them by giving them a neat little conflict resolution formula to follow. Though I'm sure he was not against using biblically consistent techniques, they were secondary in importance. He knew that conflicts primarily develop and remain unresolved among Christians because they focus on the picayune things that divide rather than the more significant things that unite them. So Paul calls the attention of these feuding women back to the central, crucial issue of what they have in common in their union with Christ.

Euodia and Syntyche may have had different personalities, interests, backgrounds, and perspectives on a lot of things. But they were both in union with Jesus Christ. It was that union that made peace and harmony possible on a practical level.

Situations similar to that of Euodia and Syntyche frequently occur in families. Again and again I have heard warring family members say something like this: "We have nothing in common. Our personalities clash. Our interests, desires, and expectations are different. Even our likes and dislikes make us incompatible. We just can't get along."

Yet I have seen these ugly walls come tumbling down when family members have been willing to exchange their focus on the things that divide and annoy for a primary focus on their relationship with Jesus Christ. When it comes to conflict resolution, there is nothing more important, more practical, and more helpful than a vital relationship with Jesus. Notice that I said a *vital* relationship with him. There are many Christians who, while having a relationship with Christ, do not have a really vital and deep relationship.

Some time ago, I talked to a woman who was having serious difficulties with her husband and her work associates. Her talk and demeanor indicated that she was very selfish, demanding, critical, and hard to get along with, but she took no responsibility for any of the difficulties. Since she claimed to be a Christian, I asked her what that meant. She gave me the standard answer, and I continued: "Well, let me ask what difference Jesus Christ makes in your life on a day-by-day basis? How did Jesus influence your relationship with your husband today? What difference did Christ make down at your job yesterday?"

She answered, "I don't go down to the job and lie and cheat, as some of the others do." "That's good," I replied, "but you could probably find a lot of non-Christians who don't go around lying and cheating on the job."

She went on to tell me about some of her other good behaviors, such as, "I don't go around swearing and cursing." Again, I acknowledged that while avoiding profanity is desirable for Christians, there are a lot of non-Christians of whom the same could be said. So, I reiterated, "I want to ask you again, what difference does Jesus Christ make in your life?" Finally, she responded by saying, "I don't really know that he makes any difference in my life on a practical level."

This woman had been raised in a professing Christian home, had always gone to church, had accepted Jesus into her heart as a child, and had adopted an external lifestyle reflecting her church's standards. She sang in the choir, occasionally read her Bible and prayed, went to a Bible college, and married a young man from the same school. Many of the trappings of external Christianity were in place. But her relationship with Christ was very superficial. He wasn't personal or real to her at all.

Did this superficial relationship with Jesus Christ have anything to do with her interpersonal problems? To answer that question, let me reemphasize: when it comes to conflict resolution, there is nothing more important, nothing more helpful, than a vital relationship with Jesus Christ. When every family member is experiencing a growing, vital relationship with Christ, the potential for incredible harmony exists for a number of reasons.

Unity Through a Common Standard

Substantial unity is possible among people who have a common standard for making decisions. When Christians come to me with marriage or family problems, I'll often say to them, "Tell me what it means to be a Christian." Many reply, "A Christian is someone who has believed on the Lord Jesus Christ."

"You're absolutely right," I respond. "'If you confess with your mouth Jesus as Lord, and believe in your heart that God raised Him from the dead, you shall be saved' is what Paul wrote in Romans 10:9. Now, what do you think the Bible means by confessing Jesus as Lord?"

"It means that Jesus is sovereign. He's in control of everything in the universe."

"Yes, that's right, but what does it mean for you personally to confess Jesus as Lord?"

After people have made a few attempts to explain what it means, I usually turn to the white board in my office and say, "Let's spell *Lord* in a different way." Then I write in big letters *Boss!* "On a personal level, for you to confess Jesus as Lord means that you acknowledge that Jesus is your Boss." Then turning to each family member, I inquire, "Have you acknowledged Jesus as your Boss?"

After they all have affirmed that Jesus is Boss in their lives, I say to them sincerely and enthusiastically: "What you've just confessed is great news in terms of resolving the problems that bring you to counseling. If all of you have the same boss and want to do what he wants you to do, then we can expect to see this situation resolved. He's not going to give confusing directives by telling one of you to do something that conflicts with what he tells the other. Right now, since you're having conflicts, one or more of you must not be listening to orders from the boss. In resolving your problems, your main concern shouldn't be what you want, but what Christ wants in your relationships. Now, what do you think Christ wants you to do about your various difficulties?"

A poor, illiterate man was converted when he heard the gospel at a rescue mission in a large city. He continued to attend Bible studies there. One night everyone else in the room was wearing sweaters with writing on the front. After the meeting he went home and said to his wife, "I'd really like to have a sweater with words on it." His wife agreed to knit him one, but she couldn't read either. Finally she decided to copy the words she saw on a restaurant window across the street. When it was finished, her husband proudly wore it to the Bible study.

At the meeting, people commented appreciatively about the message on his sweater. Its words perfectly described what happens when a person becomes a Christian. The sweater read, "UNDER NEW MANAGEMENT."

That's what a Christian is—someone who has come under new management. A Christian is a person who has confessed Jesus Christ not only as Lord of the universe but as Lord of *his life*, and who is submitting to the implications of that lordship in the practical details of life. If every family member has acknowledged Jesus as Boss, his will as revealed in his Word becomes the common standard by which decisions are made and differences are settled. In such a family, people may not always agree about what the Scriptures mean or how they apply. But they will have a basic agreement that the Scriptures—not their own desires or opinions—are the final authority. If, therefore, family members disagree on the meaning or application of Scripture, submission to the Boss will encourage them to wait on him for greater insight into his will. In such families Christ functions as the peace officer whose standards provide a solid base for preventing and resolving family conflicts.

Unity Through a Common Purpose for Living

In homes where Christ's lordship and presence are living realities, he operates as a peace officer by providing a common purpose for living. The reality of Christ's love becomes a compelling force that lifts people above their own self-centered concerns to live for him and his purposes (2 Cor. 5:14, 15). When Christ's love—expressed in his living, dying, rising, and ruling for us—becomes a treasured, abiding reality in our experience, many of the disagreements we have with other people seem insignificant. We become caught up in a cause far bigger and far more important than any of our petty concerns. Our hearts are broken and filled with the love of Christ. In response, we say with John the Baptist, "He must increase but I must decrease" (John 3:30).

When Christ is real to us, we see him as our greatest possession, as Paul did in Philippians 3:8: "I consider everything a loss compared to the surpassing greatness of knowing Christ Jesus my Lord, for whose sake I have lost all things. I consider them rubbish, that I may gain Christ" (NIV). When we are in vital union with Jesus, our heart's desire is to see him exalted. Getting glory for ourselves or having our own way loses its appeal. Seeking first the kingdom of God and his righteousness becomes our greatest concern. When we recognize the higher cause in which we as believers are involved, it's amazing how speedily our perspective changes on the importance of some of our differences. Christ pulls us together in our commitment to purposes more significant than the little things on which we disagree.

Unity Through a Common Enablement

Christ performs his work as the peace officer every family needs by filling their lives with a sense of contentment, strength, and security. Many of our conflicts in the home develop because we are trying to derive from our family relationships what we should be receiving from God alone. We are looking to family members for our security, satisfaction, affirmation, and contentment. That is precisely what God accused the religious people of Jeremiah's time of doing. "My people have committed two evils: They have forsaken Me, the fountain of living waters, to hew for themselves cisterns, broken cisterns, that can hold no water" (Jer. 2:13). Whenever we look for contentment and security in family members, we are forsaking the fountain of living water and digging broken cisterns that cannot hold water.

Paul's reminder in Colossians 2:10 that we have been made complete in Christ is right on target. Objectively, in our standing before God, we have everything we need because we are united to Christ. God has declared us righteous and views us as faultless. All of Christ's perfect righteousness has been credited to us. Because of our union with him we need no other righteousness to make us acceptable to God.

Our completeness in Christ, however, goes beyond this objective aspect. Christ came that we might begin to experience a subjective kind of completeness also. He intends to change our condition as well as our position. "I came," said Jesus, "that they might have life, and might have it abundantly" (John 10:10). "If any man is thirsty, let him come to Me and drink. He who believes in Me, as the Scripture said, 'From his innermost being shall flow rivers of living water'" (John 7:37-38). When we are living in a vital, personal relationship with Christ, we experience a sense of subjective completeness. God gives us an inner strength so that we can say with Paul, "I have learned to be content in whatever circumstances I am" (Phil. 4:11).

Family members often become argumentative and emotional because they feel threatened. Underlying their sinful responses is a sense of emptiness and insecurity that they are trying to overcome through the approval of other people. They interpret disagreement as disapproval. In an attempt to overcome their own felt deficiencies, they overreact to differences and seek to coerce family members into agreement in order to recover security. The resulting compliance makes them feel good because they have tied their sense of worth to the approval of others.

In such cases family members have forgotten that they are already complete (sufficient, adequate) in Christ. Those who live in vital relationship with Christ don't need to dominate other people. They don't have to coerce others into agreement in an attempt to bolster their own self-image. They are already fulfilled, sufficient, and complete in Christ even if no one else in the family agrees with them.

Our worth and satisfaction doesn't come from those around us. It is imputed to us in the same way our righteousness is. Any value we have is a gift because of our relationship with Christ. In union with him we have also been blessed with the indwelling presence of the Holy Spirit, who will make us like Jesus Christ and empower us to fulfill God's calling for our lives, regardless of the opinion people may have of us. The approval, agreement, and appreciation of other family members is nice, even desirable. But it is not an absolute necessity because in Jesus Christ we have everything we need to live.

A Family That Needed a Peace Officer

What happened in Ken and Dorothy Martin's (pseudonyms) family is a living testimony of how Christ performs his peacemaking work. At approximately age twenty-eight, Ken and Dorothy went to a foreign mission field with an enthusiastic desire to make an impact for Christ in a primitive culture. Upon their arrival they worked hard to learn the language and adapt to the culture. Eventually they were stationed with a veteran missionary couple to do pioneer mission work. Ken and Dorothy moved to their post with great delight—they were doing what their hearts yearned to do.

Occasionally they would become upset with one another or the children. Ken would do or say something Dorothy didn't like, Dorothy would offend Ken, or the children would misbehave. This would lead to a discussion, which would intensify into an argument. Ken would become verbally aggressive, and Dorothy or the children would usually become very hurt and retreat into silence. Ken would use strong-arm tactics to get his wife to see his point of view or his children to obey him.

Dorothy would then dissolve into tears and, for the sake of peace, give in even though she often didn't really agree. The issue then was swept under the rug—they would "kiss and make up," pray, and determine that they would not allow themselves to act this way again. But, inevitably, something else would come up, and they would revert to the same kind of behavior.

The frequency and intensity of these conflicts escalated. It became obvious to the other missionary couple and eventually to the field director that the Martins had serious family problems. Attempts to help them on the field were unsuccessful, and they were ordered to return to America for counseling.

Ken and Dorothy knew the Scriptures well and were serious about their Christian faith. They were aware of what they should and shouldn't do. Yet they didn't have the power to implement what they knew was right. Both of them were discouraged, confused, angry, and ashamed. They very much needed Jesus Christ to be the peace officer who would restore harmony to their home.

During our counseling we explored many areas of their lives and relationship. We identified the areas of conflict and sought to understand how they had developed. I became aware that Ken and Dorothy had been sidetracked from a focus on Jesus Christ in their lives and relationship. I was convinced that their problems evidenced not only a breakdown in their relationship with each other, but also a deficiency in their relationship with Christ. They had become so caught up with their problems and responsibilities that they had lost their Christ-centeredness.

I knew they couldn't resolve these difficulties on their own. They had already tried many times and failed. Somehow they needed help in developing a more vital relationship with Jesus, who could provide for them a unifying standard, a unifying purpose, and a unifying contentment and enablement. In the course of counseling, I gave them many different kinds of assignments. All were meant to bring them into a more vibrant relationship with Christ.

According to Dorothy and Ken, the one assignment that was more helpful than any other was to study passages of Scripture about their union with Christ. I gave them a list of such passages and asked them to note their implications in terms of their relationships with God and with family members. Most of the verses were very familiar to them, but as they focused on them from the perspective I had suggested, some verses took on a new significance.

Commenting on what several passages in Romans 5 and 6 meant in terms of his relationship with God, Ken observed:

> These verses indicate that I no longer need to worry about God's wrath or judgment. God does not continue to hold my past offenses against me. He freely and fully forgives me and accepts me because of Jesus Christ. I do not have to atone for my own sins; God doesn't make me pay for my wrongs; he doesn't rant and rave at me and hold me at arm's length. My standing before God is always founded on his grace communicated to me through Christ, not on my works of righteousness or my perfect agreement with him. My right of access to God is always my union with Christ, not my own merit. In Christ I have the blessed hope of ultimate, eternal salvation, and I can and should live in the joy of that assurance. My future is a glorious one. Because of Christ, I have reason to rejoice in tribulation. The God who has accepted me freely and fully will use every trial I experience to do something good in my life.

As he applied these same passages to his family relationships, Ken reflected further:

In my relationship with family members, I should not dwell on past offenses and failures. I should forgive them freely and fully because they are in Christ and because God has forgiven me and them. I should treat my wife and other family members not according to what I think they deserve or merit, but by grace I should extend to them my love, attention, and understanding. Since Dorothy and I share the same assurance and joy, it should affect our relationship as we rejoice in the same salvation. My reaction to trials that may come to me through other family members should be one of joy and hope because God will use them to make me more like his Son.

My hope of glory is certain. Nothing my family does can take it away. I need to be and can be a more joyful person because of Christ. My joy is not dependent on the perfect performance or agreement of my family. This is a principle of life that I have forgotten to practice over the past few years. That neglect is no doubt a root problem in our marriage. I have been convicted of it several times in this past week. I need God's grace to begin afresh, to die to sinful, selfish desires and rights, to live this blessed newness of life through the resurrection power of Christ.

As counseling progressed, the Martin's discouragement and anger abated. Significant changes came in their attitudes and behavior toward God and each other. Things that had bothered them previously didn't seem nearly as important. A new respect for one another developed. Lines of communication began to open, barriers started coming down, and old conflicts were discussed and resolved. Several months after counseling ceased and their relationship continued to make progress, the mission board allowed them to return to the field.

What was the primary factor that helped these people to resolve long-standing and bitter conflicts? I asked Ken and Dorothy that question as we concluded our counseling sessions. Their answer: being called back to the centrality and vitality of their relationship with Jesus Christ. During counseling, Christ called them back to himself. Once again they focused on knowing him and making him known. As that happened in their lives, Christ broke down the barriers of enmity that had grown up between them.

What I've written may sound simplistic to some of you. Maybe it seems too pat, too abstract, too mystical. I assure you it is not.

Hundreds of people like Ken and Dorothy illustrate its practicality. If you want to overcome conflicts in your family, don't allow yourself to become so focused on the conflict that you are diverted from Christ. Make sure that you focus on knowing, serving, and pleasing the Lord. Depend on him for your security, recognizing that you are complete and sufficient in Jesus Christ. Acknowledge his authority. Reflect on his great love for you, and accept the fact that your completeness is found in him (Col. 2:10). Absolutely nothing is more practical than that!

Study and Application Assignments

Do the assignments individually and then discuss your answers with your mate or your study group.

1. Describe your reaction to the content presented in this chapter.
    a. Did you agree or disagree with what was presented?
    b. Was there anything particularly encouraging or discouraging?
    c. Explain how the content may be applied in your own life or used in helping others.
2. This chapter indicated that the union Christians have with Christ provides the basis for our union with each other. Do you agree that this union provides a powerful basis for conflict resolution? Why or why not? Support your response with Scripture.
3. If our union with Christ provides us with a powerful basis for peace in the family, why do disagreements turn into conflicts and why does discord escalate between family members?
4. In this chapter I stated that some conflicts arise and remain unresolved because a person feels insecure, powerless, and insufficient. Explain how these personal judgments and feelings promote conflicts and hinder conflict resolution.
5. What were the specifics of the counsel Paul gave about conflict resolution in Philippians 4:2, 3?
6. In what three ways did this chapter indicate that Christ functions as a peace officer in families?
7. What did this chapter indicate it means to confess Jesus as Lord?

8. Can you think of cases in which people with serious disagreements were drawn together by their commitment to a greater cause?

9. How do the following verses relate to conflict resolution?

   a. Colossians 2:10

   b. Philippians 4:10-13

   c. Jeremiah 2:13

   d. Psalm 27:1

10. Study the following passages and note the words that suggest the possibility of having a personal (as opposed to a detached) relationship with God.

    a. Psalm 27:1-10

    b. Philippians 3:8-10

    c. Ephesians 3:16-19

    d. 1 John 1:3

    e. John 15:1-16

    f. Romans 8:15

    g. Ephesians 2:13-22

    h. Hebrews 2:11

    i. Hebrews 13:5, 6

    j. Isaiah 41:10

    k. Psalm 23:1-6

    l. Matthew 5:8

    m.2 Timothy 4:17

    n. Psalm 27:4

    o. John 17:3

    p. 2 Timothy 1:12

11. What does it mean to have a "personal relationship with Christ"? What are the similarities and differences between having a personal relationship with another human being and with God? Study the following verses and notice what they say about the nature of true friendship, i.e., what they suggest about deep personal relationships.

    a. Psalm 35:13, 14

    b. Proverbs 17:17

c. Proverbs 18:24

d. Proverbs 22:24, 25

e. Proverbs 27:6

f. Proverbs 27:9

g. Proverbs 27:10

h. Proverbs 27:17

i. Ecclesiastes 4:9-12

j. Genesis 5:22

k. John 15:13, 15

l. Job 42:10

m. Song of Solomon 2:16

n. James 2:23

o. Matthew 11:28-30

p. Hebrews 2:10, 11

12. What limitations or qualifications does the fact that we are not yet in heaven put on our relationship with God? What may we reasonably and biblically expect in terms of a relationship with God this side of heaven? How will our relationship with God be different in heaven than it is now? Why is this important to remember? Consider the implications of such verses as:

a. Psalm 16:11

b. Psalm 17:15

c. Psalm 63:1-8

d. 1 Corinthians 13:12

e. 2 Corinthians 5:7, 8

f. Ephesians 1:13, 14

g. Philippians 1:21-23

h. Philippians 3:10

13. How does a deep personal relationship with Christ develop? How is it hindered? Reflect on how a deep personal relationship develops with any person. What encourages such a relationship? What may hinder its development? Especially think of Bible passages that shed light on how to get to know Christ. Here are a few examples:

a. John 5:39

b. John 14:21, 23

c. John 15:1-16

d. Matthew 5:8

e. Romans 8:15, 16

f. 2 Corinthians 4:6

g. 2 Corinthians 6:16

h. Ephesians 3:16-19

i. Colossians 3:16

j. 1 John 1:6

k. Revelation 3:20

l. Joshua 1:8, 9

m. Psalm 27:1-14

n. Psalm 46:10

o. Psalm 63:1, 2

p. Isaiah 55:6, 7

q. Isaiah 57:15

Summarize your conclusions about how to develop a personal relationship with anyone. Then apply what is legitimate to developing a personal relationship with God.

14. Evaluate the depth and vitality of your own relationship with Christ on a scale of 0-4.

     4__ = almost always vital and personal.

     3__ = frequently deep, real, and personal.

     2__ = now and then deep and personal.

     1__ = seldom deep or personal.

     0__ = I have never known what it is to have a personal
          relationship with God.

15. Complete these sentences:

a. My personal relationship with Christ has been hindered by . . .

b. To develop and maintain a deep personal relationship with God I must or will . . .

Notes

[1]John Gwyn-Thomas, *Rejoice Always* (Edinburgh: Banner of Truth, 1989), pp. 13-15.

14

Turning Family Discord into Concord

A little girl who had been playing with friends came home with her head down and a scowl on her face. "People, people, people," she muttered under her breath. "What's the matter, honey?" her mother inquired. But the little girl ignored her, went to her room, and closed the door. When her father knocked on her door and asked, "May I come in?" the girl replied: "Go away! I don't want to see you— you're a people too." She was learning at an early age that relating to people isn't always pleasant or easy.

Relationships with others can be an extremely fulfilling aspect of life. Scripture affirms, "Behold, how good and how pleasant it is for brothers to dwell together in unity!" (Ps. 133:1). Unfortunately, we all know from personal experience that there's another side to this story. Probably more tears have been shed over bad relationships than any other single factor. It is extremely rare to find someone whose greatest struggles are not with other people.

Virtually nothing is more unpleasant than fighting and hostility among family members. The prophet Malachi describes people who weep and groan because of problems in their marriage (Mal. 2:13-16). The book of Proverbs also draws our attention to the grief and heartache caused by problematic family situations. Children can be the source of excruciating sorrow for their parents. Parents can bring distress to children. Marriage partners can make their mates so miserable that they want to run away to the wilderness (Prov. 10:1; 17:21, 25; 19:26; 20:7, 20; 21:9, 19).

Nothing can affect our walk with God and our service for Christ more than the way we get along with family members. In his classic passage on godly marriage relationships, Peter highlights the fact that following his directives is a matter of concern to God. To wives Peter says in effect, "Being the kind of wife I've described not only will make you a powerful influence in the life of your husband; it will also be precious in the sight of God" (1 Pet. 3:1, 4). And to husbands: "Being the kind of husband I've described not only is important for your marriage; it's also important to God. If you don't treat your wife in this God-ordained way, your prayers will be hindered" (v. 7).

Paul underscores this same connection in Colossians 3. In the early part of this chapter he gives general instructions about the kind of life Christians should live. Verse 17 concludes this section with a broad exhortation: "Whatever you do," Paul writes in effect, "must be done under Christ's authority, as his representative, with his approval, and to his glory." In verse 18, Paul begins to work out the specifics of what it means to live this kind of life. Significantly, this portion commences with a description of how Christ wants family members to relate to one another. The gist of Paul's instruction is this: "Doing what you do in Christ's name will involve the ways that you as husbands and wives, parents and children relate to one another. You will be good representatives of Christ as your family functions in a God-ordained way." Thus, learning how to resolve inevitable family disagreements is not an option, but a necessity for anyone who wants to build his family God's way. Happily for us, God has given us practical guidelines for turning family discord into concord.

Biblical Guidelines for Family Concord

In my estimation, Ephesians 4:1-3 is one of the greatest passages in the Bible on the subject of resolving conflicts. When I compare it to the family conflicts I have experienced or observed, I never cease to be amazed at its depth, comprehensiveness, and practicality. Here Paul writes,

> I, therefore, the prisoner of the Lord, entreat you to walk in a manner worthy of the calling with which you have been called, with all humility and gentleness, with patience, showing forbearance to

one another in love, being diligent to preserve the unity of the Spirit in the bond of peace. (Eph. 4:1-3)

R. T. Archibald noted that "peacemakers . . . carry about with them an atmosphere in which quarrels die a natural death."[1] When certain people are around, contention seems inevitably to spring to life. When other people are present, conflicts tend to diminish. What characterizes people in whose presence conflicts die a natural death? They manifest five qualities mentioned by Paul in Ephesians 4:1-3. They are (1) diligent, (2) humble, (3) gentle, (4) patient, and (5) forbearing.

Peacemaking Qualities

Diligence

When Mary and Dirk came for counseling, Dirk's approach to two important areas of his life stood in stark contrast. He was a very successful physician with a large family practice. To achieve this status, he had spent many years in school, followed by an extended period as an intern and then as a resident physician. Finally Dirk and Mary had moved to an area of the country in need of physicians, and he had begun his family practice.

In his profession Dirk spared no effort. He worked long and hard and soon developed a favorable reputation around town. Because of his skill and his dedication to doing whatever was necessary to help people, his medical practice grew. That, of course, meant more work for him, but Dirk didn't mind. In fact, he seemed to thrive on it. Laboring sixty to seventy hours a week was no problem. Developing a large practice was worth any effort he could make.

Unfortunately his approach to his marriage and family life was quite different. At home he expected to be treated like a king. His wife was to be at his beck and call, shaping her schedule around his. Dirk couldn't be bothered with home responsibilities. He made almost no attempt to deepen their relationship through shared activities or constructive communication. When Mary would try to discuss important issues in their family, Dirk would accuse her of being unreasonable and retreat into stony silence. Yet in his eyes, he was the ideal husband.

After fifteen years Dirk decided that he didn't want to be married to Mary anymore. "No," he said, "I'm not in love with anyone else. I just don't want to be married to Mary. She expects too much and she will never change. I want relief from the pressure. I'll be better off without her and so will our son." In counseling, Dirk said: "Marriage is not at all what I expected it to be. We have too many problems. Mary is too different from me. If I had known that marriage was going to be like this, I never would have gotten married." When challenged about the need to work at a marriage, Dirk responded, "If you have to work hard at it, it's not worth it."

Like Dirk, many other people will do whatever is necessary to get ahead in their chosen occupations, but they are unwilling to put forth the same kind of effort in the home. When it comes to family life, they are lazy, expecting that good family relationships will develop automatically. They have the fairy-tale idea that a godly, peaceful house is the result of magic or chance rather than laborious effort. As a result, their families are torn apart by a maze of unresolved conflicts.

According to Paul, keeping peace in or out of the family will require diligence and dedication (Eph. 4:3). You must be willing to make every effort and give it all you have.

Humility

The words "with all humility" found in Ephesians 4:2 point to a second characteristic of the peacemaker. God's attitude toward humility and its opposite—pride—is highlighted in many passages of Scripture. Isaiah tells us that God chooses to dwell in a unique way with the contrite and humble of spirit (Isa. 57:15). Two New Testament verses inform us that "God is opposed to the proud, but gives grace to the humble" (1 Pet. 5:5; James 4:6). On several occasions, Jesus Christ declares, "Everyone who exalts himself shall be humbled, but he who humbles himself shall be exalted" (Luke 18:14; cf. 14:11; Matt. 23:12).

The Proverbs contain numerous warnings against proud people, as well as promises to the humble.

> Everyone who is proud in heart is an abomination to the Lord; assuredly, he will not be unpunished. (Prov. 16:5)
>
> The fear of the Lord is the instruction for wisdom, and before honor comes humility. (Prov. 15:33)
>
> A man's pride will bring him low, but a humble spirit will obtain honor. (Prov. 29:23)

No one can read these passages of Scripture and doubt that pride is a deterrent to our relationship with God. Pride also interferes with our relationship with people. According to Proverbs, "When pride comes, then comes dishonor, but with the humble is wisdom" (Prov. 11:2). Proud people tend to treat family members disrespectfully. Because they put other people down, it's easy for others in the family to develop an adversarial attitude toward them.

A proud person seeks his own honor, considering himself to be filled with wisdom, someone whose insights should be sought after and highly regarded. Instead, as Proverbs says, he finds dishonor. It is hard to respect someone who has an exalted view of himself. We're inclined to want to disagree with such a person. "Pride only breeds quarrels" (Prov. 13:10, NIV). So when you find yourself in conflict with other family members, carefully consider the likelihood that pride is affecting your relationships.

The humble take seriously Christ's warning about being judgmental (Matt. 7:1-5). But the proud are quick to shift blame, assuming in any conflict that the other person is all wrong, or at least mainly wrong. The humble person so fully acknowledges the plank in his own eye that the faults of others by contrast seem to be mere specks. When contention arises, he examines himself: "I know how sinful I am. I'd better start by examining myself. What wrong attitudes do I have? What unwholesome words have I spoken? What unChristlike actions have I displayed? Where am I in error?"

Humility enables one to take full responsibility for his own wrongdoing without blameshifting, rationalizing, or covering up. The prodigal son displayed such humility when he returned to his father and said, "Father, I have sinned against heaven and in your sight; I am no longer worthy to be called your son" (Luke 15:21). He didn't say to his father: "I'm sorry for what I did when you were too domineering and overbearing. I shouldn't have treated you the way I did when you tried to prevent me from doing what I wanted to do." He didn't justify or rationalize what he had done. In humility, he took full responsibility for his attitudes and actions.

When family discord arises, we can often find some fault in what another family member said or did. It may even be that we were wholly undeserving of the other person's treatment. At that point, pride says, "I'm justified in what I think, do, or say because the other person started it." But humility impels us to the opposite response: "Two wrongs don't make a right. Two wrongs just make two wrongs. I can't excuse sinful behavior or blame it on someone else. I am fully responsible for my actions regardless of what is done to me."

Humility will display itself by our asking for forgiveness when we have wronged another person. When I counsel couples, I frequently hear the charge, "He [or she] never asks for forgiveness." One husband stated that in twenty years he had never heard his wife speak those words. "Is that true?" I asked her. She replied, "You don't have to ask for forgiveness unless you've done something wrong."

Imagine that! In twenty years of marriage this woman could not think of one thing she had done wrong! With this self-righteous attitude it's not difficult to understand why the couple's disagreements had proliferated.

Mike came for counseling after his wife had run off with another man. Other people had told Mike: "Forget her! You're better off without her." For some reason, Mike wasn't ready to do that. He wanted to make sure that he had done everything he could do to restore the relationship, and so he decided to seek help. After he had poured out his heart and we had prayed together, he asked me, "What do you think I should do?" I said, "Mike, my opinion is no better than anyone else's. If you wish, I'm going to tell you what I believe God wants you to do. Is that what you want?"

He agreed. Sensing that he was emotionally ready to receive

some straightforward teaching, I turned to Matthew 7:2-5. "Mike," I said, "whenever others hurt us, we usually focus on their wrong-doing and nurse our hurts. That just seems to be the right thing to do. But in this passage Christ is telling us to do otherwise. He says that we ought to begin by examining ourselves to see what we have done wrong. I know that may seem unfair because you didn't leave your wife, you didn't run off with another woman, but it's still what I think our wise and loving Lord is telling us to do. He's not saying there isn't a time and place to deal with your wife's sins, but he is saying that you should begin by looking at your own wrongdoing before you focus on hers. Do you think that's what Christ is saying here?" Mike agreed and I went on to ask, "Are you willing to do the hard, painful work of examining where you have failed as a husband and father?"

"I want to do whatever Christ wants me to do. I know that there are many ways in which I've failed her, my children, and God. Over the years, my dental practice has often come before my family. I was selfish and inconsiderate. Judy tried to talk to me about her concerns, but I told her she ought to be satisfied because I was a much better husband and father than many other men. I've been a Christian for many years, but I've allowed my own spiritual life to suffer. At times, convicted about my lack of spiritual leadership, I made some small, temporary changes. But then I'd slip back into my old ways."

I gave Mike time to review his own "logs" and then encouraged him to confess his sins to God and receive God's forgiveness through Christ. Then I told him that I wanted him to do something that might be very hard, something that would take a lot of humility. "I want you to contact your wife and confess to her the specific ways in which you have failed. I want you to ask her to forgive you and tell her that with God's help you are going to change. I don't want you to preach at her or tell her what a wicked, horrible sinner she is. Focus on getting the 'logs' out of your own eye.

"I can't guarantee how she will respond. She may refuse to forgive you and throw what you say back in your face. She may deny any wrongdoing on her part. But I still believe it's what God would have you do. Will you do it?"

Mike committed himself to doing this, and he left determined to clean up his own act. He contacted his wife, confessed his sins, and asked for forgiveness. Judy was astonished. Previously, he had always defended himself and blamed her for the problems in the marriage. Now, he was taking full responsibility for his failures.

God used Mike's genuine display of humility to disarm Judy and break down the wall of resentment she had developed. He repented, then she repented and returned to her family. Together they came for counseling to deal with the issues between them. And together they worked through them until they developed new patterns of relating to each other. For Mike and Judy, real changes began to take place when he was willing to humble himself and exercise diligence in their marriage.

Gentleness

The much neglected and often misunderstood quality of gentleness is a third factor in the Bible's peace program (Eph. 4:2,3). In biblical times, the Greek word translated "gentleness" was sometimes used to describe a tame animal. Think of the implications of this for interpersonal relationships. A person who lacks gentleness is like a wild animal. When applied to family relationships, Paul's point about gentleness is unmistakable. Families disintegrate when parties in the home bite, devour, and rip each other apart. Such savage behavior produces apprehension, defensiveness, and closed-mindedness as family members attempt to protect themselves from injury. In this atmosphere, conflict resolution is very difficult.

Behaving like a gentle, tame animal produces the opposite effect. When people know that we will not hurt them, they cease being defensive. In the presence of gentleness, family members are more prone to really listen to what we're saying. Disagreements are less likely to become emotional issues in which saving face takes prominence. Power struggles are diminished and reasonable discussion can occur because respect and sensitivity is shown for one another.

Paul calls us to be like our Savior, who was gentleness par excellence (2 Cor. 10:1). Jesus was "gentle and humble in heart" (Matt. 11:29). He didn't go around quarreling, yelling, shouting at people, and embarrassing them. He was not insensitive to their hurts and weaknesses, using his superior intellect and oratorical ability to argue them into submission. Instead, he was careful to treat them with tenderness, sensitive to their feelings and condition. With astonishing care and gentleness he ministered encouragement and strength to them (Matt. 12:18-21).

This kind of spirit displayed so wonderfully in Jesus has amazing peace-keeping power. The absence of gentleness will turn disagreements into conflicts and make conflict resolution very difficult, if not impossible. But gentleness is a powerful tension-reducing agent with a capacity to draw people together.

Patience

"When it comes to patience, my scorecard reads zero," I recently heard a church leader admit from the pulpit. I appreciated this man's honesty, but his casual laughter, which followed, led me to think he didn't consider this deficiency to be very serious. Yet according to the Bible, patience is an essential Christian character quality. The apostle Paul treats patience as a prerequisite to unity and peace with others (Eph. 4:2, 3).

Because a patient person is slow to become angry or annoyed, he does not over-react to disagreements. His calm demeanor defuses potential conflicts (Prov. 15:18, NIV). Under pressure, the patient person averts or mitigates offenses with his composure (Eccl. 10:4). He doesn't immediately display his irritation when attacked (Prov. 12:16; 19:11). He doesn't return evil for evil. Rather, committing himself to him who judges righteously, he seeks to respond in a way that would please God and help other people (1 Pet. 2:21-23; Prov. 15:1, 28).

Resolving differences doesn't always happen quickly; frequently it takes time and can be uncomfortable. We don't like to have someone oppose us. We want instant agreement, and when we don't get it, we may become impatient and refuse to discuss the issue any further. We forget that attaining harmony is a process, not an instantaneous event.

Impatience prompts people to use counterproductive strategies to avoid controversial issues. Stubborn silence, tears, threats, topic shifting, blameshifting, busyness, insincere compliance, and staying away from home are all destructive techniques that hinder the resolution of family conflicts. Patience on the other hand makes us willing to do the hard, sometimes unpleasant work of discussing and praying about conflicting perspectives until we are able to reach agreement.

"Be patient," says James, " . . . until the coming of the Lord. Behold, the farmer waits for the precious produce of the soil, being patient about it, until it gets the early and late rains. You too be patient . . ." (James 5:7, 8). The farmer doesn't plant the seed and then expect to reap a harvest the next week. Having put the seed in the ground, he fertilizes, waters, and cultivates it—and waits. He knows that poking at the seed will not help it grow more rapidly. So he does what he can, and then waits.

James's concept of patience has tremendous implications for conflict resolution. Family members need space to consider our ideas without undue pressure. Not all changes in thinking or behavior occur in a hurry. We must be content to allow some changes to develop gradually. Family relationships are hindered and conflicts intensified when we fail to realize that some changes will take time. Husbands and wives who communicate rejection and superiority by demanding immediate transformation of their mates' character or behavior will only produce discord in their relationships. Parents who will not allow their children to mature gradually will foster a combative spirit in their family.

Forbearance

Closely related to patience is the character quality called forbearance. In one sense it is a facet of patience—you can't have one without the other. Nevertheless Paul in Ephesians 4:1-3 singles out forbearance for special emphasis. He thereby highlights the key role this facet of patience has in preserving unity.

Concerning the need for this quality, Jerry Bridges writes:

> People are always behaving in ways that, though not directed against us, affect us and irritate or disappoint us. It may be the driver ahead of us who is driving too slowly, or the friend who is late for an appointment, or the neighbor who is inconsiderate. More often than not it is the unconscious action of some family member whose irritating habit is magnified because of close association. The kind of patience it takes to overlook these circumstances is probably demanded of us most often within our own families. . . .[2]

Many squabbles develop because family members will not allow other people to make mistakes or be different without putting pressure on them. Intolerant people point out every blunder another person makes. They don't distinguish between major and minor issues. Somehow they feel that not making another person immediately aware of his blunders would be an abdication of responsibility (Prov. 19:11; 17:9).

We would do well to emulate the way our great God deals with the members of his family. Consider the forbearance of Jesus Christ with his disciples. As God manifest in the flesh, he was fully aware of all of their sinful thoughts, words, and actions. He could have continuously reprimanded them for every fault and sin. But he didn't. He carefully chose what to call to their attention and when, where, and how to approach them about issues of the greatest concern.

As I write this chapter, I have been a Christian for almost forty years. During this time, I have come to appreciate how forbearing God has been with me. I can look at my life and see how some growth has taken place by God's amazing grace. However, to my shame and sorrow, I must confess that I still have a long way to go. In many respects I am so unlike Jesus! Yet God has never given up on me. He still loves me and has always been patient with me. He doesn't excuse or condone my remaining sins, but he's not constantly beating me down about them. With great forbearance he has continued to grant me full acceptance through Jesus Christ and to work in me so that eventually I will be completely conformed to the image of his Son (Phil. 1:6; Rom. 8:29; 1 John 3:2).

I am encouraged to know that God graciously tolerates me with all my faults. And do you know what? This forbearance of God doesn't make me careless about my sin. To the contrary, God's forbearing love fosters a devotion to him that makes me hate my sin and want to please him all the more (1 John 4:19; 2 Cor. 5:14).

So it will be in our families. When we display the kind of forbearance God shows to us, we will be doing what he says needs to be done to turn discord into concord. The walls that divide us as families will begin to come down, and the cords that bind us together will grow stronger. Take to heart Paul's prescription for peacemaking. With dependence on the Holy Spirit (Gal. 5:22, 23; 2 Cor. 3:18), seek to develop the five qualities described in Ephesians 4:1-3. As they abound in your life, you will become a peacemaker in whose presence conflicts die a natural death, giving rise to greater harmony in your home.

Study and Application Assignments

Do the assignments individually and then discuss your answers with your mate or your study group.

1. In what way does Ephesians 4:1-3 indicate the importance of resolving conflicts?

2. What does the phrase "be diligent to preserve the unity of the Spirit" suggest about conflict resolution?

3. Why is an attitude of humility such an important part of conflict resolution? How will true humility display itself when we interact with family members? What will humility prompt us to do that will facilitate conflict resolution?

4. How will gentleness aid conflict resolution in the family?

5. How will gentleness manifest itself when disagreements arise?

6. What biblical passages illustrate the gentleness of Christ? What do they suggest about the way our interactions with people can promote conflict resolution?

7. Why is patience helpful in the conflict resolution process?

8. How will patience manifest itself when disagreements arise?

9. What does forbearance have to do with conflict resolution?

10. What does forbearance mean, and how will it be displayed toward others?

11. Think of biblical or contemporary people who were or are good at peacemaking without being wishy-washy in their convictions. How were the qualities mentioned in Ephesians 4:1-3 demonstrated in their lives?

12. Think of a Christian married couple or family you know who seem to have a great relationship with each other. What qualities characterize their lives? What are the reasons for their good relationship?

13. How would you rate the harmony and unity of your family? Does your family exemplify the unity of the Spirit in the bonds of peace? What is the peace quotient of your family?

    Excellent___Good___Fair___Poor___

Explain your reasons for rating your family as you did.

14. Evaluate your ability to resolve conflicts according to the criteria suggested in this chapter. Use the following criteria:

    4 = usually, 3 = often, 2 = sometimes, 1 = seldom, 0 = never

Do you:

(1) Make every effort to resolve disagreements?	4 3 2 1 0
(2) Take full responsibility for your wrongdoing?	4 3 2 1 0
(3) Avoid blameshifting when you sin?	4 3 2 1 0
(4) Ask forgiveness when you have wronged another family member?	4 3 2 1 0
(5) Recognize your own fallibility, limitations?	4 3 2 1 0
(6) Realize your understanding or interpretation may be wrong or inadequate?	4 3 2 1 0
(7) Listen carefully and respectfully when other family members speak?	4 3 2 1 0
(8) Refuse to judge or draw conclusions until you have made sure you really understand?	4 3 2 1 0
(9) Listen even if the other person is saying something you don't want to hear?	4 3 2 1 0
(10) Look at things from the other person's perspective before you answer?	4 3 2 1 0

(11) Manifest sensitivity to the feelings of others?	4 3 2 1 0
(12) Answer family members graciously?	4 3 2 1 0
(13) Put others at ease, make others feel comfortable?	4 3 2 1 0
(14) Avoid making people feel stupid?	4 3 2 1 0
(15) Practice long-suffering when provoked or mistreated?	4 3 2 1 0
(16) Hang in there when unpleasant, painful situations arise?	4 3 2 1 0
(17) Face and resolve disagreements rather than run from them?	4 3 2 1 0
(18) Give people time to change?	4 3 2 1 0
(19) Make allowances for differences?	4 3 2 1 0
(20) Distinguish between major and minor issues?	4 3 2 1 0
(21) Allow people to fail without punishing them for it?	4 3 2 1 0
(22) Respect family members even when you disagree or when they have sinned?	4 3 2 1 0

Total number of 2s: ___ (need for some improvement)
Total number of 1s: ___ (need for considerable improvement)
Total number of 0s: ___ (need for much improvement)

To fulfill Ephesians 4:1, 3 you must improve in the areas that you rated 2, 1, or 0. If you have a considerable number of 0s or 1s, your family is experiencing many unresolved conflicts and not the unity of the Spirit in the bonds of peace. If you are a Christian, you can improve. Review chapters 12–14 and design a biblical strategy for promoting personal improvement in handling disagreements and promoting conflict resolution. Complete the following sentence.

To become better as a peacemaker and conflict resolver, I will . . .

15. Study the following Scripture passages and note what each has to say about peacemaking or conflict resolution. Make applications to your own family.

    a. Genesis 13:8, 9

    b. Genesis 26:17-31

    c. Esther 10:3

    d. 2 Samuel 10:1-14

    e. Psalm 34:14

    f. Psalm 133:1

    g. Proverbs 10:12

h. Proverbs 13:10

i. Proverbs 15:1

j. Proverbs 15:4

k. Proverbs 15:18

l. Proverbs 17:14

m. Proverbs 20:3

n. Ecclesiastes 10:4

o. Romans 12:14-21

p. Romans 14:19

q. Galatians 5:13-23

r. Philippians 2:1-9

s. James 3:14-4:2

Notes
[1]Derek Kidner, *The Proverbs* (Downers Grove, Ill.: InterVarsity Press, 1972), p. 115.

[2]Jerry Bridges, *The Practice of Godliness* (Colorado Springs: NavPress, 1983), p. 209.